Emotional Energy Transformation

Emotional Energy Transformation

Siamak F. Shirazi

Copyright © 2013, Siamak F. Shirazi, LLC

All rights reserved. No part of this book may be reproduced, stored, or transmitted by any means—whether auditory, graphic, mechanical, or electronic—without written permission of both publisher and author, except in the case of brief excerpts used in critical articles and reviews. Unauthorized reproduction of any part of this work is illegal and is punishable by law.

ISBN 978-1-304-13036-5

Contents

- **Introduction**..vii
- **Chapter One**
  - Energy is Everything, Everywhere, All the Time...................1
  - Energy Never Dies; It Only Changes Form (Transforms) 2
  - Energy Systems in Relation to Human Anatomy 5
- **Chapter Two**
  - The Satellite Dish Analogy 13
- **Chapter Three**
  - The Theory of Empty Spaces..23
  - Is There Only One Energy? 25
- **Chapter Four**
  - Emotional Health and its Relation to Internal Organs 31
- **Chapter Five**
  - The Internal Energy Network and the Meridian System 39
- **Chapter Six**
  - Dan Tian Energy System and its Relation to Emotional Balance 43
- **Chapter Seven**
  - Breath-Work and Visualization 49

- o   The Power of Visualization 51
- **Chapter Eight**
  - o   Connecting, Cultivating, and Utilizing Your Energy 55
- **Chapter Nine**
  - o   Exercises for Specific Feelings and Individual Organs 83
- **Chapter Ten**
  - o   Conclusion – Excerpts from Patient Conversations 125

Contents

- Introduction vii
- **Chapter One**
  - Energy is Everything, Everywhere, All the Time 1
  - Energy Never Dies; It Only Changes Form (Transforms) 2
  - Energy Systems in Relation to Human Anatomy 5
- **Chapter Two**
  - The Satellite Dish Analogy 13
- **Chapter Three**
  - The Theory of Empty Spaces 23
  - Is There Only One Energy? 25
- **Chapter Four**
  - Emotional Health and its Relation to Internal Organs 31
- **Chapter Five**
  - The Internal Energy Network and the Meridian System 39
- **Chapter Six**
  - Dan Tian Energy System and its Relation to Emotional Balance 43
- **Chapter Seven**
  - Breath-Work and Visualization 49

Introduction

Emotional Energy Transformation simply means that we have the capability to transform (change) our emotional state if we can just understand and relate to our feelings based on the concept of energy movement within our body.

I will make a clear comparison between Eastern philosophy, which is rooted in the *balance* of our emotions, versus Western analysis, which is based on the *observation* of our emotional expressions. The Eastern viewpoint stems mostly from an inherit wisdom of countless generations and the deep interconnection between the mind/body and its organic environment. The Western understanding relies heavily on the observation of our reactions to events which take place in our surrounding environment, and their effects on our behavior.

My intention is not to condemn the Western understanding of our feelings and its available solutions to address emotional imbalances. I only wish to emphasize other available and helpful options and different ways of understanding our body. This includes the body's inner relationship between organ systems (Liver, Lungs, Heart, etc.) and emotional balance. I would like for my readers to grasp a new concept to enhance their emotional awareness and learn easy-to-apply tools to enhance their everyday living experience.

A new set of data and a different perspective will allow us to perceive consciousness in a profoundly different way. This means if we have new information that enables us to examine life in a different paradigm (or from another unexplored viewpoint), our reality will alter, and our experience of living on this planet *can* change for the better.

We are (for the most part) followers of our past perceptions. This applies to our collective consciousness and not just individual thoughts. Nations, religious and political organizations, and other organized groups of people who share a common belief, are all creating a reality that is suitable to their belief system, which provides the opportunity for their group to feel righteous. If a group of people all believe in one thing, that in itself will provide authority and legitimacy for that tenet, regardless of its origin. Whether we are talking about a political, religious, or a scientific ideology, commonality will provide a group with a sense of legitimacy and the authority to support their argument. Each group, regardless of their agenda, will produce a set of data to which they can "collectively" relate. To them, that idea is factual and speaks their truth. Therefore, that truth will affect the quality of their experience and shape their reality, regardless of its background, or, in some cases, its logical deficiencies.

From a scientist's perspective, this planet has been turning around the sun for millions of years, and gravitational forces can be explained by simple laws of physics. The scientist's belief system relies heavily on observation of factual and tangible events, drawing legitimacy from a set of well-defined and understood scientific rules. Yet to some religious believers, the earth was made in 7 days and about 5,000 years ago. Each group has the same level of conviction in their belief system, and is able to produce data and evidence which supports *their* argument. There are many people who also believe in both of these ideas. There are well known scientists who also have passionate, yet unscientific, views about topics that science falls short in explaining.

There are hundreds of other viewpoints, and to their believers, each one has some validity and represents a relevant interpretation of reality. I am not supporting any one argument over the other. To me, the most important aspect of the human experience relies on the awareness (or the lack of awareness) of our surrounding environment in relation to our own body. The quality and depth of our experience in Western culture is closely connected to external stimuli. What takes place "outside" of our bodies usually defines how we behave and experience reality. The way we are perceived by others or the outside world is paramount in shaping our behavior in Western culture. As a result, we usually lack self-awareness and are mostly disconnected from our bodies. We normally refer to our bodies as a third party when we speak of our ailments, or our shape, or our place in the world. We perceive "I" as an anti-matter thought system, deeply buried within our brain cells and our consciousness, and completely separate from our skin cells, or the liver tissue, or any of the internal organs.

Why does it only take a few seconds for us to "feel" upset if we are exposed to sad news or have an argument with someone we care for? And why does it only take a few seconds for us to "feel" improved when we are given a warm smile by the same person? The emotional transformation between these opposite feelings is what most interests me. I would like to expand our innate ability to alter our current emotional state, and ultimately, our reality. This process has always been based on our common wisdom, subtle guidelines and/or messages which create our collective consciousness. Thus, introducing a new interpretation of our experience will become necessary to alter our reality. What I would like to propose is a new paradigm to explain our emotional fluctuations in a different light. I want to increase the quality of our everyday life experience and emotional well-being.

Being deeply connected to our own bodies while undergoing any experience, and feeling in control regardless of our surrounding environment and external stimuli, is my main objective.

Throughout my personal journey of self-discovery, I came to realize that the answers to some important yet basic questions like, "Who am I?", "Where have I come from?", "What makes me truly happy?", could change based on my emotional state at the present time. We as humans tend to have a more positive outlook on life when our bodies are functioning well and we are experiencing emotional contentment. On the other hand, we normally have a darker perspective on life when we are dealing with physical and/or emotional ailments and feel disconnected with our bodies.

My goal is to help alleviate our emotional state (regardless of our surrounding environment) by offering simple-to-follow guidelines for being more in touch and better connected to our bodies.

There are numerous stories and historical evidence about individuals who were able to alter their feelings and "create" their own reality regardless of their surrounding environment. People who have been war prisoners or held captive in extremely dire circumstances due to natural disasters were somehow able to use their deep internal resources to cope and survive unimaginable situations. The same resources are available to us all, at all times, and we don't need to be in extreme circumstances to utilize them. This book can provide you an easy access to tap into those deep inner resources.

Chapter One

I.

Energy Is Everything, Everywhere, All the Time

Basic physics provides us with simple theories that can be used to make sense of everyday life experiences. These theories are provided as "laws" that govern the entire universe (as we know it), and can explain how things function and/or shape the way they are. One of the laws that I would like to expand upon is the law of physics that says, "Energy is *converted* from one form to another, but it is never created or destroyed." Simply stated, energy never dies; it only transforms (changes form). It basically means that energy is in a constant state of transformation at all times.

This basic law of energy transformation can also be applied to the state of our emotional health, if interpreted physiologically. There are many biophysical processes taking place every second within our bodies. Biochemical substances and bioelectrical processes are constantly transforming energy inside and outside of every cell to provide nutrients and to dispose of unused materials for our bodies to function. This process is changing and is affected constantly by many known and many unknown factors.

From the point of view of a physicist, every atom of a living cell can be described as a 99% empty space, or a huge empty void, within which subatomic bundles of energy are travelling at the speed of light. And at the quantum level of subatomic particles, all matter can be described as literally "frozen particularized energy fields," or "frozen light." Therefore, complex collections of matter (molecules) could also be interpreted as small clusters of energy, or energy fields. Just as light has particular frequencies, so does matter have frequency characteristics. The less dense or subtle the matter, we find higher frequencies of light within that matter. Thus the physical cells and molecules (or all matter) could be one form of energy manifestation when light vibrates at a lower frequency. And everything less tangible, or, if you will, "non-matter" (like emotions and feelings), is manifested when light vibrates at much higher frequencies. Therefore, one can argue that our emotions and feelings, even thoughts, are figuratively transformed back and forth from the nonphysical (not tangible) state to the physical (cellular) state via transportation of light and the change of its vibration and frequencies. In other words, how one person experiences life, perceives pain, and responds to pleasure, can be vastly different from another person simply based on their biochemistry alone. I will discuss this in more detail in upcoming chapters and talk about other factors (social conditioning, genetics, etc.) that also play significant roles in the way we each perceive reality differently.

II.

Energy Never Dies—It Only Changes Form (Transforms)

There are millions of transformations within our bodies at any given hour. The timing, accuracy, and environment of these transformations are important factors that can shape our experience of everyday life. They can be influenced by things as obvious as our nutrition or exposure to pollution, or things that are less obvious such as a breakup of an emotional bond (e.g., divorce), or the death of a loved one. All these influential factors can determine the entire quality of a human experience and define its outcome.

The cell population of our body is swimming and living within what's called "interstitial fluid" (or tissue fluid, or intercellular fluid). This is a solution that surrounds the cells of all multi-cellular beings. It is the main component of the extracellular fluid, which also includes plasma and transcellular fluids. This playground, or internal cellular universe, has an important role in the health and proper function of every cell within our body. I strongly believe that its role becomes more crucial when it's concerning our neurons or the cell structures of our nervous system. Very basic and simple knowledge of how nerves communicate and relay messages throughout their network will provide important information about the relations between interstitial fluid and nerve cell functions. The entire identity or quality of a message *can* be altered based upon the environment in which the nerve cells are swimming. Although all our neurons are protected with an insulation layer called the myelin sheath[1], there is a very small gap (a synaptic gap), or what is called "neural synapses," that remains exposed between the nerves. It is in this very small space full of interstitial fluids that a message "jumps" from one nerve cell to another.

Of course, this all occurs at mind numbing speeds, and usually it takes less than a second for a signal to travel from our fingertips to our brain and back. But the message still needs to jump between every cell via these synaptic gaps. This process has as much to do with electricity as with chemistry. The messages magically jump between cells like tiny lightning rods, and it is in that moment, that very short period of time, that the interstitial fluid can alter and affect the nature and even the signature of that message. This might happen in a very subtle way, but nevertheless it's very possible that the environment in which this spark takes place does interfere with the content and the quality of the message.

To illustrate my point, imagine a group of athletes quickly passing a basketball to one another. Everything on that basketball court can and will affect the ball's speed, force, and accuracy. If the room is very cold or too hot, if the floor is wet and slippery, if there is direct light coming into the players' eyes, outside noise, etc., the ball will be affected. The environment in which they are working is affecting their productivity. The same theory could apply to the relationship between passing neural messages in synaptic gaps and the environment of the interstitial fluid.

---

[1] **Myelin** is a dielectric (electrically insulating) material that forms a layer, the **myelin sheath**, usually around only the axon of a neuron. It is essential for the proper functioning of the nervous system.

One demonstration of the importance of synaptic gaps is the discovery made by scientists at the University of North Carolina at Chapel Hill School of Medicine. They have shown that one of the elements required for the nerve cell connections to form and function correctly is a protein called neurexin which releases at the synaptic gaps as one nerve cell is communicating a message to the other. Their discovery of this protein and its role as a neurotransmitter, made in Drosophila fruit flies, may lead to advances in understanding autism spectrum disorders (recently, human neurexins have been identified as a genetic trace risk factor for autism). The study does not imply that the appearance of this protein alone is a known cause of autism; however, it can increase the risk of this condition in an individual. This is just one small demonstration of the importance of synaptic gaps, how a message travels through our nervous system, and its direct effect on our behavior.

As I mentioned earlier, energy is *converted* from one form to another, but it is never created or destroyed. The entire process of a message being transmitted within our bodies from one neuron to another is a great example of physiological energy transformation. I believe that an energetic process similar to the physiologic process of touching a hot iron happens within our body when we meet a new person. There are constant messages travelling back and forth within our bodies, and information is being exchanged and interpreted. The fact that we sometimes feel very close (or the opposite) to someone when we meet them for the first time has to do with this process of interpretation and perception from their energy to ours. This is why, in most cultures, people make some kind of an instinctive physical gesture, or connection, when they meet. In many western cultures, we shake each other's hands as a greeting. This transformation of information works similarly to the synaptic gaps between the nerve cells, and it exchanges information and energy signatures.

I also believe that our thought process, or what I like to refer to as our "information management system" and the manifestation of our reality, is also the result of a transformation of energy. Thus, when we have a healthy environment for the energy to transform internally, we have a much more precise and clear message to interpret from a situation or another person. The only way we can truly manage the effects and outcome of any situation is by changing (transforming) our own perspective and reactions. We can choose to enhance the accuracy of this internal process (energy transformation system) to have an easier time processing the information, and to have a more accurate response.

III.
Energy Systems in Relation to Human Anatomy

Getting to know and connecting with our bodies from the energetic point of view is the key element for achieving emotional balance. The same principle applies to any system. One needs to first study the structure and foundation of a system before you can understand its function. There are several different explanations of humans' energy systems. The most popular in the West perhaps came from the Indian culture and the first Yoga enthusiasts who either came from India or travelled and trained there.

The idea of improving one's health and enhancing their internal energy via Yoga practice started to receive attention in the Western world during the early sixties. Millions of people in the U.S. are now avid yoga practitioners and followers of that early adaptation of an ancient eastern culture. They benefit from the philosophy of mind/body connection through a set of physical movements and use it to enhance their everyday life experience.

Chakra system

You might have already heard the term "Chakra", but may not be familiar with its true meaning. There are seven Chakras located within the energetic boundaries of the human anatomy. The word Chakra is Sanskrit and translates as "wheel" or "disk", and signifies the seven basic energy centers in the body. Each of these centers also correlates to some of the major nerve ganglions[2]

---

[2] In neurological contexts, ganglia are composed mainly of **somata** and **dendritic structures** which are bundled or connected. Ganglia often interconnect with other ganglia to form a complex system of ganglia known as a **plexus**. Ganglia provide relay points and intermediary connections between different neurological structures in the body, such as the **peripheral** and **central** nervous systems.

branching out of the spinal column. There are theories that chakras also correlate to different levels of consciousness, archetypal elements, developmental stages of life, colors, sounds, and more.

Dan Tian system

The Dan Tian (DT) system is extensively used in all forms of Martial arts, Chinese Medicine, and Qi Gong practice. There are three main energy centers, or hubs, in this system rather than seven. The DT system and its branches relate to the maintenance, transformation, and transportation of the energy within our bodies. I will explore our three Dan Tians at length in the upcoming chapters, but for now, here is a brief overview:

- The first Dan Tian, or the base DT, is the lower energy center located in our lower abdominal area, about 2 1/2 inches below our navel and about halfway between the front wall of the body to the back wall. It could be perceived as the combination of the first, second, and third Chakras. The lower DT is what keeps us physically balanced and centered, and it provides us with the sense of being grounded within our physical body.
- The second or middle DT, which is located within our chest cavity, is mostly involved in managing our feelings and emotions. It is the first point of contact for all the emotional energy which enters our body, and it is how we connect with others emotionally. It could also be perceived as the combination of the fourth and fifth Chakras.
- The Third or higher DT is closely related to our intellect, imagination, and sense of creativity. Imagine it as a hyper sensitive, supper connected hub to what's beyond our physical experience of everyday life. It could also be perceived as the combination of the sixth and seventh Chakras.

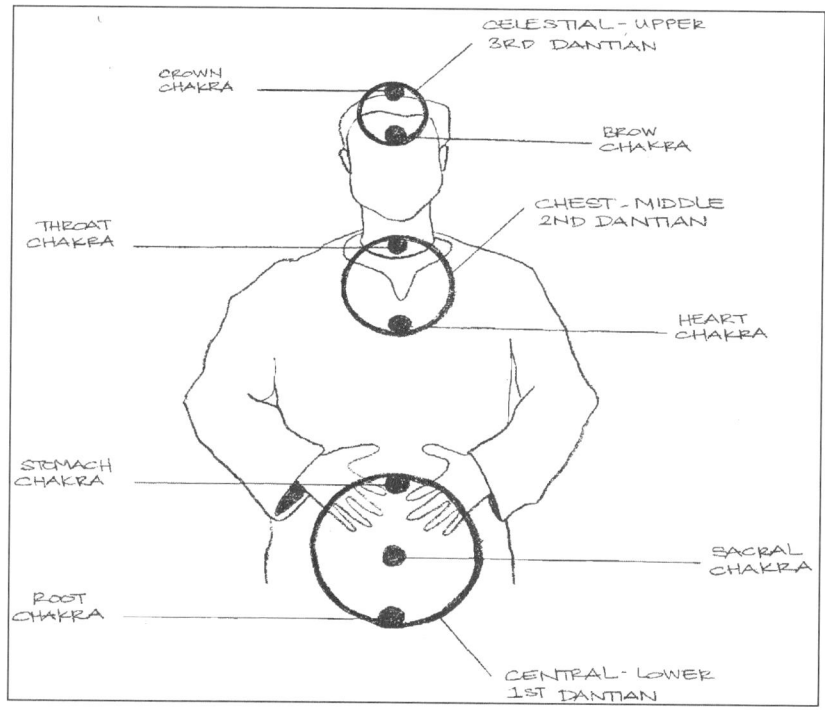

Figure A

A brief visual study of these energy systems (Figure A) will reveal that they line up alongside the Central Nervous System (CNS) from bottom to top. They may be perceived as spheres or energy fields surrounding, circling, or wrapping around the spinal column, and on top, the brain, which is the main hub for our CNS. They may vary in size and shape based on different sources, but their placement and general area of influence within the body is well defined in all sources, from several thousand years past to the current time. The most important aspect of a DT is its function as a center which is receiving and transforming the energy that travels through our bodies.

Both the Chakra and Dan Tian systems correlate directly with the CNS, however the Dan Tian model also extends to the peripheral nervous system via the expansion of energy meridians (Figure B) It is through this network that we can observe the main overlaps between the entire nervous system and energy movement within our bodies. The receiving of information via our senses, the brain's

Emotional Energy Transformation

interpretation of our sensations (sensory function), and our reactions and/or physical movements (motor function), are all closely dependent upon both the central and peripheral nervous systems. Since there is a close link between these two systems, understanding and working with our energy system becomes as critical as understanding and working with our nervous system. Furthermore, knowing the energy system and its function within our bodies will introduce us to a different and more tangible paradigm. It will offer a view to an intimate relationship with our bodies and the way we handle the messages we receive from our senses, feelings that we experience, and thoughts and actions we deliver.

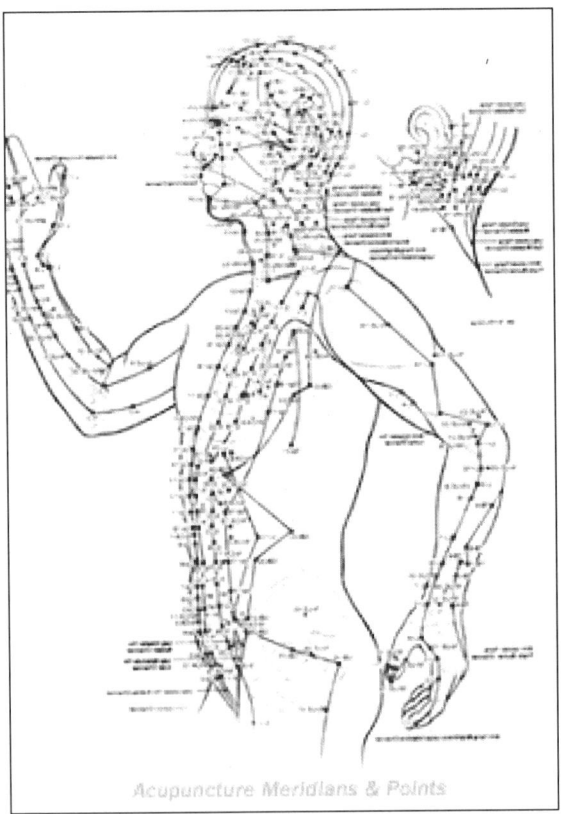

Figure B

Every feeling that we experience can be observed not only as a neurological and physiological phenomenon, but also an energetic event. We need to expand our minds and be able to reach beyond the mainstream physiological understandings of our senses and perceive our sensations as energy transformation events. We already know that energy is only *converted* from one form to another, but it is never created or destroyed. We can easily apply the same "law" or principle to internal sensations that we experience on daily basis through our feelings. That's why we can be moved within seconds from one state of mind to another, from one sensation to another, and our living experience is altered simultaneously. We can be very calm and within seconds switch (transform) to excitement or anger. We can be in a sad state, and with just one thought, one sentence, a sound, or a smell, we can be moved to joy and bliss in a heartbeat.

These subtle changes happen via complex neurological, chemical and physiological activities within our bodies. It has taken many years of close scientific observations and research to help understand some of the physical aspects of all these changes. I value the Western views of our bodies since it places significant importance on observation of our physical manifestation (the physical body) and makes great efforts to observe and record physical and tangible changes. However, since our living experience is truly an internal perception/interpretation of the external environment, I am proposing another option for making sense of the way we react and behave. This different paradigm is not to "replace" the Western physiological views and psychological analysis. But it can complement all the extensive findings and research that is taking place in regards to our senses and feelings. And that is the paradigm of Emotional Energy Transformation.

A closer study of our body's energy systems reveals important information about some of the basic physical and neurological sensations we feel. As energy travels through our body, it can change form and shift from one state to another. And as we get to know that system better, we can then affect an alteration of these transformations to achieve better physiological, emotional, and energetic balance.

The first step is to understand and relate to our feelings from the energetic point of view. This is accomplished by learning specific techniques which allow us to connect with our own energy centers more effectively. I reveal the *physical* locations of our energy centers within the body, and then I will expand and discuss easy techniques to visualize and connect with them. We then begin the active and mindful cultivation and utilization process of our own ever expanding, internal energy resources. Within this framework, and by learning these easy to use techniques, we can grow and *expand energetically*. This will allow us not only to feel calmer and more grounded inside, but also to affect our surrounding environment.

Every single thought contains information: **information is thought, in formation**. Every thought contains energy in some form, but its awareness is usually beyond our conscious level. I think that's one reason why, thousands of years ago, people started to believe in the power of prayer. We probably knew on some unconscious level that our thoughts carry a great deal of energy. Perhaps a better illustration of the power within our thoughts is what I referred to at the beginning of this book as "collective consciousness." If a group of people strongly believe in something, with enough time, focus, and meditation, that thing (for that group) becomes reality. Our collective thoughts can give rise to events; our current predictions, visions, and stories can shape our future.

The fact that we have the need to predict the future and make up thoughts in the first place has perhaps a lot to do with our past, which once was "the future" at a time before it, and so on. The entire universe in which we experience our existence is a massive pool of information manifesting at different rates based upon variables like time/space gamut. This means the current manifestation of the information which we experience as reality now can be a product of a thought process in the past. That thought process was stemmed and also affected by the information, but in the raw form. The raw form of information is the true energy that we need to access, connect with, and draw from, all within our own bodies. The unfiltered, unaltered, and universal energy which isn't influenced by our belief systems is what I like to call our "core energy", and that is the aim of any energy cultivation program, prayer, or meditation. Learning about and finding that internal source of power is the first step toward cultivating our energy and, later, learning how to transform it. I believe that a true healing experience takes place with the involvement of our "core energy", whether it is through an extensive internal struggle and/or training, or a breakthrough which can be caused or influenced by another source (field) of energy.

When we practice active meditation or Qi Gong (a Chinese form of medical meditation), we are trying to slow down our unending internal conversations. The internal conversation is the processing mechanism, and it is creating our perceptions from the universe and also shaping our responses and expressions. Our internal conversation starts very early on as we are fed with "synthetic" information. "Synthetic" information is all the ideas and terminology which we learn from our surroundings and people. The reason I like to call it synthetic is because of its distance from that "core energy", or the blueprint and information which exists within our own body. Most of the training and conditioning we receive as we are growing up is the fruit of our collective consciousness.

Our entire belief system has been passed on through generations with limited modifications. Basically, we still believe in almost everything we did thousands of years ago, but we are justifying our beliefs differently today compared to a few thousand years ago. As we feed our newborns with this information about life outside of their bodies, we divert their attention from life within. Quite early on, we start a busy internal conversation for them to process all the external information, which truly distracts them from the peace and quiet they could inherently feel inside - and we call this process of conditioning teaching or training.

Humans have been conditioning their offspring this way for thousands of years; thus most of our conflicts, arguments, and wars are still happening for the same reasons as they did several centuries ago. We may have advanced greatly with technology in the past several decades. We may have become more connected with one another and better informed about our surrounding universe, but intellectually and energetically, we are not wiser as a species. We have a lot more information to process but are not wiser in handling and processing it. We force feed the same type of belief systems to our newborns without examining the effectiveness of these old ideas towards any holistic and global improvements. The cause of most of our massive and global conflicts are still rooted in very old world views, thus we shouldn't be surprised that our world is behaving in those same old ways today.

Chapter Two
The Satellite Dish Analogy

The reality which we experience in our daily lives is the mere *interpretation* of the reality which is constant for the universe around us. People referred to this phenomenon as the "internal world" vs. the "external world". I like to refer to it as "personal reality" in relation to "general reality". The general reality constitutes the collective consciousness, like a known law of mathematics. It should be perceived, understood, and utilized in a very similar fashion for anyone.

The personal reality however is very unique to the individual and varies from one observer to the next. It is subjective and can be argued according to different participants' viewpoints. The way we experience the world emotionally is unique to our own senses and their interpretations. It's a lot more fluid and in a state of constant flux rather than a known lucid mathematical law. As we go through life, our entire being is actively involved in a three part process:

1. We observe, feel, and receive information
2. We interpret, analyze, and perceive the information
3. And finally, we act or react based upon our perception

Observation - Feeling

A mini-dish satellite system that is typically used for home installation has three components: the circular or oval dish that they mount on the outside of the building, the receiver "set top" box that they usually place on or near the television set, and the viewing device or TV. The mini-dish is usually mounted outside to be exposed to all the signals that are on its pathway (the observation phase). It has no judgment or pre-selection, and it simply transports all that it receives to the set top box. The same thing happens as we go through life. During the observation phase, we expose ourselves to massive amounts of information based on the direction and the path we choose to travel. Although one could argue that we have limited control over the information which we are exposed to based on our circumstances (the country and family into which we were born, for example).

It is mostly in this observation and feeling stage that the millions of mini-dishes out there (if pointed toward the same direction) receive the exact same amount and type of information. We all go through the same observation phase every day as we are constantly bombarded with the same information. One thing that has changed dramatically in regards to the human condition (which will have a detrimental effect on the future) is the speed, amount, and quality of information that we receive. People who live in cities around the world are now exposed to many times more information every second, thus there are more seeds for endless internal conversations. Some are referring to this phenomenon as "information overload" or "sensory overload", which will usually force us to react more quickly and makes our reactions more sensational. There is simply *not* enough time to receive and process the information deeply and to produce calm and wise reactions to daily events.

We are faced with increasing levels of information overload in our daily lives. It is directly affecting the ability to make clear and accurate decisions, even about simple tasks, and its outcome is the unavoidable increasing of our stress levels.

Part of the problem of being exposed to excess amounts of information in a relatively short period of time is processing and analyzing all that information accurately. The other issue is the constant interruptions which can result in a lack of adequate focus. These daily interruptions include incoming e-mail messages, phone calls, instant messaging, etc., which break the mental focus and redirect it to the source of the interruption. We usually can't ignore a ringing phone or a chime of receiving new e-mails or text messages. In many cases, the interruption influences our concentration and even completely diverts our attention from the task at hand. We then have to redirect our attention back to the original task and usually retract our work back at least a few seconds. In 2005, the research firm "Basex" calculated the annual cost of unnecessary interruptions and related recovery time at $588 billion in the U.S. alone. That figure was updated to $650 billion in early 2007, and it is continuously growing.

Interpretation - Analysis

It is in this stage, when the information starts being analyzed and interpreted (perception phase), that the receiver set top box plows through the massive amount of information and sorts based on your "pre-programmed" package. You could have chosen an all action package or soap opera channels, etc., and based on your previously made choices, the set top box will select the "right" type of information to pass though.

This stage is where the collective consciousness has the biggest impact on the viewing by-product. A large number of us can have the exact same viewing package and thus will end up perceiving and analyzing information similarly.

Politicians usually use this knowledge as a very effective campaign strategy. They repeatedly go over a single issue that is perceived (preprogrammed) and is imbedded into our consciousness. As discussed in my introduction, collective conciseness within large groups of people creates tailored world views that can act as effective *perception filters* for political propaganda. It is with the help of different *perception filters* (culture/society, religion/ideology, parenting/conditioning, etc.) that we each create a unique, yet similar world view for any given archetype. A person who was severely abused as a child, for instance, will automatically (usually unconsciously) use that *perception filter* to analyze the information they receive to create a world view. This view may have many similarities with the view of another person who was abused at a similar age, but in a different family, and even within a different culture. However, every experience presents with *personal* aspects, unique to that individual.

Emotional Energy Transformation

Action - Reaction

Finally the picture is viewed on our television set based on the type of packaging that we have purchased and what our set top box is receiving. The picture we see is a representation of reality, as our perceptions make that determination, based on our individual *perception filters,* in real time. For instance, when we are watching a live sports event or a music concert with a group of people, it is much easier for us all to have a general idea about what is actually taking place in that real physical location at the same time. But when the same group is watching a movie, the actual perception of what is taking place becomes more individualized as it gets filtered through more perception filters.

It is becoming more difficult, especially for the younger generation, to distinguish between what's *real* and what is "real". Television and electronics are becoming major sources of information and produce interesting perception filters from a very early age. Distinguishing between what is actually real, on a "reality based" game or TV show, is increasingly difficult for the younger generation. There are also documented cases of subliminal advertising on television dating back to as early as 1950, although that is whole topic unto itself.

I remember watching television or a movie as a child growing up in the late sixties and early seventies. There was a clear distinguishing between an actual live event and other pre-produced programming we watched. My parents took the extra effort to let me know that what I was watching was pretend reality and not actuality - especially during a graphic and violent scene when actors were shot or a speeding car was thrown off the cliff, for example. I am not sure if parents are making the extra effort to explain the difference for their children nowadays. Usually the best they do is to plan ahead and make sure that their kid is not watching an "R" rated movie or a graphic program.

Since television and pretend reality has been around for a few generations now, parents might automatically "think" that the distinction (which my parents had to provide) has somehow become a part of our psyche, and children are inherently able to tell the difference. Plus, many parents don't realize that even all those "G" and "PG" rated events are also full of confusing messages and use subliminal messaging to connect kids to certain products or a particular lifestyle.

We can truly believe in different world views from the same perspective, or the same view from different perspectives. For example, two people with different ideologies or beliefs may have the "same" level of convictions and even be willing to die or kill for their beliefs. Or, real events in one person's life may appear to be more like a fantasy in the others'. This last phase of interpretation and analysis is what creates our life experience, and it's strongly shaped by our preprogrammed perception filters. Changing our viewing package takes reprogramming, or what Steve Covey[3] likes to refer to as a *paradigm shift*. It is through this change in our perception and transformation that we allow ourselves to truly "see" the potential within.

Not too long ago I was listening to a radio interview. It was a program about intense human experimentation and testing, and how some people have subjected themselves to extreme conditions for the sake of science and medicine. I remember listening to one of their interviewees explaining her experience. She was supposed to live blindfolded for a long period of time (several days as I recall). The most striking part of her interview was when she described the first few minutes after they took off her blindfold. I could hear and feel the excitement in her voice as she was explaining her experience. She was saying that the scientists and observers took her into a room, turned all the lights out, and closed all the blinds. They also covered her head with a thick white towel before they asked her to slowly remove the blindfolds while still under the towel. She said that even before she slowly opened her eyes, it was truly like a different world; viewing the towel in front of her face, even with her eyelids shut, she said it was very bright. As she started, very slowly, opening her eyes

---

[3] **Stephen R. Covey** (born October 24, 1932 in Salt Lake City, Utah) wrote the best-selling book, *The Seven Habits of Highly Effective People*. Other books he has written include *First Things First, Principle-Centered Leadership*, and *The Seven Habits of Highly Effective Families*. In 2004, Covey released *The 8th Habit*. In 2008, Covey released *The Leader In Me—How Schools and Parents Around the World Are Inspiring Greatness, One Child at a Time*. He is currently a professor at the Jon M. Huntsman School of Business at Utah State University.

and removing the towel in front of her face, she first looked at her own hands and legs. Her body was glowing like it was illuminated from within. She said that it was as if she had florescent lights in her extremities and body parts. She was *seeing e*verything so bright and illuminated in that very dark room. It took her some time to slowly return to "normal" and start *viewing* things the old way. What she experienced is what's referred to as a "paradigm shift": an opening, an opportunity to be able to perceive the world from a different perspective, and under a different light.

We are so consumed by our everyday chores and routines that an opportunity like that only presents itself after removing our physical bodies from the "normal" daily life experience for a long period of time. We are literally not able to "see" all aspects of our existence as long as we follow the same path and live in the same paradigm as our previous ancestors. Normalcy is important since it brings a sense of homogeny between humans, and we typically function better in less chaotic and more common grounds. However, it will also close many different perspectives, or windows to new possibilities, which could help us grow in *all* directions and according to our true potentials.

It is as if we own a vehicle that can travel all terrains (like so many of us in the U.S. do), and in most cases we spend a good amount of time and resources to keep it maintained and ready, but we never take it to a steep hill, let alone off-roading. The way most of us are experiencing life is like that very equipped, very capable SUV that only rides on safe, familiar and paved roads, and mostly from one familiar destination to another. Our true potentials can be put to the test only when we create the right environment for them to expand and grow.

I believe that there is an inherent desire for our senses to feel, see, and smell new territories. However, there is also the need to feel safe and grounded in a familiar environment. The balance between these two poles can create healthy growth. Leaning excessively toward either one can cause disturbance or boredom. Just as when a child is exploring and learning about his or her surrounding environment by constantly touching, looking, and experimenting, we adults need to also be constantly curious and full of questions. The day that we feel we have all the answers is the day that we have stopped growing.

Think about it: our bodies physically grow to a certain size; this is affected by so many factors like genetics, nutrition, and environment. After it reaches its maximum physical growth point, it starts a deterioration process which we still call "growing" old. This simply means that we really never stop growing, our growth just changes directions. The phrase that I used many times throughout this book, *transformation,* applies perfectly to our aging process. We are truly transforming from the moment we are conceived to the last breath we take. This transformation process goes through several different phases, but it never stops.

Unfortunately, I don't believe the same thing happens to our psyche as we acclimate to our modernized lifestyle. The need to search and discover is getting nourished by pointless web or TV channel surfing, and the desire for being grounded in a familiar environment is being fulfilled with our one dimensional living. Going to work on the same superhighway every day, performing similar tasks during the same hours, coming back home and repeating the same familiar cycle, day after day. Our senses are factually numb, and that's probably why some people tend to move toward extreme physical experiences with the abuse of drugs, sexual experimentation in not-so-safe situations, or erratic eating behaviors. All these can become habit forming since they do stimulate deeper layers of our consciousness and scratch beneath the old, familiar, and "boring" surface.

A paradigm shift is going to provide us an opportunity for awareness of energy transformation, and perhaps influence its directions and end results. Imagine being angry or very upset with something, and regardless of the cause, try to imagine what your body is going through. Your heart beats faster and stronger, your blood pressure elevates, your sympathetic nervous system is in full force, and your face is flushed. You probably are both speaking louder and hearing clearer, and your sweat glands are more active. All these changes are happening within moments from the time you first hear an argument, receive bad news, or watch a losing team during a sporting event—or whatever it is that upsets you. These changes (transformations) happen physiologically, psychologically, and also energetically. In fact, if we truly shift our attitudes and viewpoints, we may be able to perceive *all* the changes as energy transformation.

As I mentioned earlier, most of these intense physiological processes happen via electro-chemical reactions within our cells; everything is truly transforming. Now imagine that you stop the same argument I just referred to with the realization that it was a misunderstanding, or that the bad news was just a tasteless joke from an annoying friend. All these processes will change within moments. Your parasympathetic nervous system kicks in immediately and slows your heart rate. Your blood pressure drops within seconds and your body goes back to functioning calmly. This transformation happens because of the realization that you are not in danger or in need of any aggressive reaction, and thus you can relax. These sympathetic vs. parasympathetic nervous system reactions have been called *fight and flight* vs. *relaxation phases*.

Now imagine being able to have the ability and capability of not only perceiving your external stimuli (argument, bad news, etc.) differently, but also having the insight and wisdom of transforming your physiological state from fight and flight to relaxation while in the middle of a very heated argument, or upon receiving genuinely bad news. That's what they normally call "control" in psychological language, and therapists spend countless hours teaching their clients techniques for coping with stress and controlling their reactions. That type of psychoanalysis happens on an intellectual level and can be very beneficial in the right environment, and after months or usually years of practice. It is a conscious process of understanding the root cause of our behavior, intellectualizing our actions, and analyzing our reactions. However, as most of us know from firsthand experience, when it comes to emotional matters, we tend to forget most of these techniques right at the crucial moment when we are in the middle of a heated argument, or exposed to strong stimuli.

Again, I am not trying to undermine the effectiveness of psychotherapy and its role in creating a civil society. And I am *not* a trained psychotherapist. However, I don't think its accessibility is practical for the masses, and the results are usually an intellectual understanding of a certain pattern or behavior, but not an energetic (emotional) transformation. It usually involves the intense process of self-realization and delves into old childhood memories to identify patterns, and works on eliminating the repetition of the same mistakes over and over again. It's usually quite extensive and also expensive to reach ideal results. I believe providing the right opportunity for one to reach individual awareness about his/her energetic potential takes less time and could be more effective in mass or group applications. The entire process will become less *personal* in dealing with the minutiae of one's past mistakes, yet more intimately effective in regards to tools for better experiencing *now*.

Chapter Three

I.

The Theory of Empty Spaces

There are many references in the Eastern philosophy of Sufism about the similarities between experiencing an internal sense of emptiness and feeling closer to the divine power. The concept of emptiness or nothingness, "HEECH", is referenced in many of thirteenth century Sufism's poetic or explanatory writings as both the object of their practice, and also the source of inner peace and essentially what they refer to as the presence of God within. In many cases they refer to the practice of chanting and rhythmic movements as tools to achieve internal solitude, purity, and the enablement of "seeing" what they refer to as "HAGH", or God. A similar concept can also be found in the practice of Taoism or Daoism. The Chinese character for Dao represents a never ending path. To many practitioners of Taoism, this can also be interpreted as the true meaning of life being a *continuously transforming journey* with no physical destination (a journey to nothingness.) Again the same concept of enlightenment and its relationship to a lack of objectives and internal emptiness overlaps in Indian culture and in TM (Transcendental Meditation.) It is known to be the main source of calming the mind and freeing oneself from the constant internal conversations in order to connect and be in the moment.

We can also see references to this concept in many teachings of Judeo-Christian religions. The idea that solitude and seclusion have significant importance in enabling one to connect directly with God is present in most ancient cultures and spiritual practices. However, I believe that the concept of solitude has been generalized and mainly misinterpreted in some of the mainstream religious ideologies. There may be references to lack of physical and/or sexual connections with another human being (or self in the case of sex) as the source of spiritual enlightenment. I believe that all these references stem from a similar and internal instinct, or wisdom, which in many cases got confused in translation.

Based on quantum physics, almost everything consists of huge empty spaces in which very small particles travel at mind-numbing speeds. I believe that instinctively it is this empty space to which most religious philosophies and past mystic literature have been referring. It is this huge empty void that is modeling the entire universe as we know it. The cellular, internal cellular, molecular, atomic, and subatomic levels can easily resemble the planetary models of the galaxies and the "external" universe. That's why mystics like Rumi make clear references between what keeps our internal body's order and what keeps the order of the universe:

"If the wheels of my existence
give up from turning
I will return to order
by that who revolves the universe"

In reality, it's all a matter of perspective when we call something big or vast vs. small or limited. From the perspective of a molecule inside a heart valve, the valve is as vast as a country, the heart a planet, our chest a galaxy, and the body is a universe. So much is happening at the cellular and molecular levels within our bodies that it can easily resemble a universe. If we observe the mentioned heart valve tissue under a microscope (depending on the sensitivity level of the microscope) we'll find cells that are constantly busy with interacting, moving, working, living, and dying, just like a large metropolitan city. Now if you hold the same heart valve in the palm of your hand and look at it without a microscope, you'll see no movement and just a solid mass, a piece of reddish/purple fibrous tissue.

The same observation is true in relation to a piece of rock versus this planet, our planet versus the solar system, the solar system versus the Milky Way, and the Milky Way versus the entire universe. From the perspective of observers light-years away from our planet, they are just looking at a lifeless piece of rock suspended (frozen) in space. On a much larger scale, we can imagine a point of view which can see the entire universe as a single snapshot; then all the planets and stars (which are only a few in relation to the size of the entire mass), are suspended (frozen) within this vast, huge empty void. From *that* perspective, all that is taking place in the entire universe can be happening all at the same time. Therefore, when we look at a living and functioning body, we need to put things in perspective to understand its multiple dimensions, just as we *try* to understand the multifaceted universe. We need to focus both on the micro-organism and the macro-organism and use both these views in respect to what we refer to as *balance*.

II.
Is There Only One Energy?

As you remember from our earlier discussions, *energy is everything, and everything is energy*. However, that doesn't mean everything is the *same* energy. It simply means that there is a similar element in everything, which is manifested in different ways. That similar element creates commonality within uniqueness. The new holographic principle and theory[4] could also help to explain this phenomenon better. As Richard Gerber, MD points out in his book *Vibrational Medicine, Handbook of Subtle-Energy Therapies*, the holographic principle explains that "every piece contains [represents] the whole."

---

[4] **The holographic principle** is a property of **quantum gravity** and **string theories** which states that the description of a volume of **space** can be thought of as encoded on a boundary to the region—preferably a **light-like** boundary like a **gravitational horizon**. First recognized by **Charles Thorn** and later proposed by **Gerardus't Hooft**, it was given a precise string-theory interpretation by **Leonard Susskind**.

In a larger and more speculative sense, the theory suggests that the entire **universe** can be seen as a **two-dimensional** information structure "painted" on the **cosmological horizon**, such that the **three dimensions** we observe are only an effective description at macroscopic scales and at **low energies**. Cosmological holography has not been made mathematically precise, partly because the **cosmological horizon** has a finite area and grows with time.

Emotional Energy Transformation

Just as a single drop of water could *represent* a vast ocean, this principle can be detected in cellular structures of all living cells. Every cell contains a miniature copy of our master Deoxyribonucleic Acid (DNA) blueprint. DNA is a nucleic acid that contains different genetic information and instructions used in the formation and functioning of all living organisms known on this planet. The main role of DNA molecules is the accurate and long-term storage of all life forms' signature information. DNA is a set of blueprints with the instructions to construct other components of cells, such as proteins and RNA (Ribonucleic acid) molecules. The DNA segments that carry this genetic information are called genes, but other DNA sequences have structural purposes, or are involved in regulating the use of this genetic information.

This means that although most humans are born with two ears, two eyes, one nose and one mouth, they may hear the same sound a little differently from one another, or they may see the same flower as having two different shades of violet. The same energy can be manifested differently based on "individual" perceptions from the same stimuli. Thus everything essentially is different manifestations of the same energy.

Imagine what a master chef can do with a few essential ingredients. He or she can create a large number of recipes from various modifications of those ingredients. From this perspective and that of the quantum theory of light vibration for the creation of particles (matter), all our emotions are also different manifestations of the same energy. Remember from the first chapter that at the quantum level of subatomic particles, all matter can be described as literally "frozen particularized energy fields" or "frozen light." Thus the physical cells (or all matter) could be one form of energy manifestation when light vibrates at a lower frequency, and everything less tangible or "non-matter" (like emotions and feelings) are manifested when light vibrates at a higher frequency or speed.

This explains why we can switch so easily and effortlessly within seconds from one emotional state or train of thought to another. It doesn't take much to make a crying baby laugh, sometimes even as he or she cries. I sometimes like to dissect the phrase "emotion" to *e-motion = energy motion = energy in motion*. Imagine a vast ocean which is constantly fluctuating (transforming) and changing.

I remember reading a contemporary Persian poet's description of the ocean. He said that if you pay close attention to the ocean, it's in a constant state of fluctuation and is never the same from moment to moment, a description that acted as a metaphor for his emotional state at the time. In fact, that comparison can be seen in various works of classic or modern poetry. A variety of writers use the wind, or a storm, or a volcano, or many other natural events to describe a changing and fluctuating emotional (internal) state. I believe that our emotions fluctuate in the same way. They are like a vast ocean of energy within us that is constantly in motion and transformation. This goes from one manifestation to the other and another...from joy to sadness to anger to bliss and to...the next emotion. When this vast moving ocean becomes too stormy, it can easily cause internal disturbances; and when it becomes frozen, it can cause other maladies like depression. As we get closer to our inner self, we start to test the water and become aware of its depth, experience the height of its tallest wave, and grasp the distance to each of its horizons. The better connected with our true inner self and the more aware we become of the energetic side of our beings, the more effortlessly we can swim in this vast and ever-changing ocean.

Psychology and all other scientifically based explorations of the human mind are heavily focused on analyzing the behavior of an individual (or in some cases a group of people), and trying to find logical explanations, which are usually based on past experiences: "People hit their children because they were hit by their parents." Please don't misunderstand my point; I have great respect for the study and the field of psychology. There are very capable and effective therapists who are actively helping individuals to cope with their mental disorders. I make routine referrals in my private practice to a few therapists who have been highly effective in helping many of my patients. In fact, when it comes to serious mental disorders, people do need to seek professional help from a well-trained psychiatrist or psychologist. However, like everything else (my theory included), there are limitations to their effectiveness and the permanency of their approach. There may be *very* successful therapists who are helping numerous couples stay together, but they may be personally struggling with their own relationships.

I am simply proposing a new approach to shift our existing paradigm about how we experience an emotional event that might offer us a different (new) perspective of our present experience. I advocate *not* repeating all those same old patterns, which can result in going through *now* miserably, because of a past mistake or misfortune. I actually think that old experiences are all necessary, and they had to play their role at the right time in order to help shape our current perspectives and to help us grow. Dwelling on the past though is one of the most "draining" positions energetically. Think about it: people are figuratively reaching down the drain of their memories from past experiences. It's a descending, downward movement of our focus and a very compromising energetic position. This doesn't mean that one has to completely forgo reviewing the past out of the fear of dealing with those unfinished or unpleasant experiences. In fact, experiencing the current situation by using your previous lessons "intuitively" could be very productive.

Think about a drop of rain. If you tilt your head back to look up as it's falling, it will drop right into your eyes and block your field of vision - if you tilt your head forward to look down as it's hitting the ground, you only see whatever is in the background (the earth beneath that rain drop) - the only good vantage point to truly view a rain drop is by keeping your head level and by looking straight ahead. Your perception from that rain drop is still altered and influenced by many internal and external factors, but if you are truly "present", your perception is only based on the emotional energy that you are feeling at the moment. If you are well-balanced energetically, your body is simultaneously using its previous wisdom as you are moving through the current experience. If you are truly "present" while going through an experience in life, your body will grasp and perceive it much differently than when you are partially (or, in some cases, completely) removed from that moment.

The individual lifestyle choices, or in the case of Western civilization, an entire culture, can be distracting to living consciously and staying present in each moment. The amount of distraction and external stimuli is so great that our energy is constantly moving from one state to another without having a chance to ground itself and grasp what each experience has to offer. Most mystic or ancient philosophies heavily emphasize the importance of slowing our internal conversation and quieting the mind. What prayer offers in many religious practices is the solitude of the mind and the opportunity to be quiet and present in the moment. In this state we can truly listen and be mesmerized by the beauty of that internal, universal, and ever-present calming melody.

I will provide you easy to use and practical tools in achieving this very important requirement for self-discovery, internal peace, and calmness of your mind. The techniques that I will discuss in upcoming chapters not only provide you physiological benefits related to each vital organ, they will also grant you the essential ingredient of self-empowerment and a deeper internal connection to your own vast resource of energy, your own personal "fountain of Qi".

Chapter Four
Mental and Emotional Health and its Relationship to the Internal Organs

Huang Dei Nei Jing is one of the oldest texts in the world and is probably the most important medical text book that was written in ancient China. Its authors and their origins are unknown, but it is known to have been written during the "Warring States" period, which spans from about 475 to 221 B.C., and it is the collaborative work of several different authors.

This ancient classic is comprised of two books, the *Suwen* "Plain Questions" and the *Lingshu* "Miraculous Pivot," which form the basic foundations of Traditional Chinese Medicine (TCM). It introduced the theory of five-element and *Yin & Yang pathology* of disease, the physiology of the *Zangfu* (vital and internal) organs, interactions between blood, the energy meridian systems, and much more. All the subsequent Chinese medical texts are built upon the foundation which was laid down by the *Huang Dei Nei Jing*.

There are numerous remarks about deep energetic connections between emotions and our internal organs in all the foundational TCM literature. What I intend to emphasize the most from this unique concept is the relationships between the five primary internal organ pairs and their emotional manifestations.

The *Zangfu* theory consists of five *Yin (Zang)* organs and five *Yang (Fu)* organs (Table 1). Each Yin or Zang organ has a function similar to that of allopathic Western medicine (i.e., heart = pumping blood). However, they also have an energetic function based on Traditional Chinese Medicine. Each Yin organ has a function which is exclusive to TCM; it also has an association with another Yang or Fu organ. These Yin and Yang organ pairs then have other associations such as their own corresponding taste, season, element, and color.

The most important aspect of a Yin organ association (from the perspective of this book) is with its corresponding emotion and spirit. (Table 1)

Table 1

Zang Yin Organ	Emotion	Paired Fu Yang Organ	Spirit
Liver	Anger	Gallbladder	Hun (Ethereal Soul)
Heart	Joy	Small Intestine	Shen (Mind)
Spleen	Calmness	Stomach	Yi (Intellect)
Lung	Grief	Large Intestine	Po (Corporeal Soul)
Kidney	Fear	Bladder	Zhi (Will)

According to Traditional Chinese Medicine, the essence and source of Ying and Yang can be interpreted as light. Ni Jing claims that these two are the main manifestations of the same energy which makes up everything that exists. As we can see in the above table, each of the main internal Yin organs has a direct relationship to one of these manifestations and a set of feelings associated with them. The Western analytical medical system is science-based. It would rather dissect things into the smallest pieces and analyze the building blocks than to view them as a whole. The Eastern philosophical medical system is primarily based on the observations of the surrounding nature and its relationship with the human body. For any analytical system, there is only black or white, right or wrong, based on the examination of minor changes in the minutia of things. However, for a holistic system which is based on a philosophy of complex interconnections within everything that exists, observations are more focused on the big picture.

Liver >< Anger - Frustration

The liver is a major organ in both TCM and the Western Medical Systems, and many of its basic functions are similar. For instance, the liver is involved in blood transportation and filtering in both systems. In TCM, the liver is described as a refiner for the quality of both Qi and Blood. The emotion anger gets expressed (manifested) when there is an imbalance of the liver organ. From the TCM perspective, that imbalance can result in the pent-up energy, or "stagnated Qi," getting constrained in the liver.

This phenomenon can work in both directions, meaning that unresolved anger as an emotional experience can affect the liver function as an organ, and physiological disease of the liver as an organ can result in the manifestation of anger. When the unresolved and pent-up anger energy is accumulating in the liver, it will contribute to what's known as "the stagnation of liver Qi (energy)." From the physiological perspective, cirrhosis of the liver, a common condition in Western Medicine, can also lead to issues with pent-up anger energy.

Since describing details of Chinese Medical terminology and pathology is not the aim of this book, I am not going to spend a lot of time explaining TCM. However, in basic terms, any liver pathology can initiate an energetic imbalance in the liver organ. And unexpressed (suppressed) anger can also cause liver imbalance. There is a famous TCM diagnoses which is referred to as *"Liver Qi stagnation (leads to) > Liver Yang Raising."* It simply means that any imbalance of the liver which results in Qi stagnation can lead to the raising of the Yang energy. This can result in an emotional episode with severe irritability or even eruptions of anger. Or it can cause other issues like migraine headaches, dizziness, ringing in the ears, and myriad other symptoms that can either manifest by themselves or accompany anger.

A common example of this phenomenon within our Western culture is the direct link between emotional imbalance and drug or alcohol abuse. Most individuals who abuse alcohol or drugs to the point of liver damage also have severe emotional issues with unexpressed (suppressed) anger and vice versa.

Heart >< Joy – Anxiety - Excitement

The heart plays a major role in the transportation of blood throughout the body. In both medical systems, its function is basically a pump that delivers fluids. However, in TCM it is known to be the "house," or place, of a type of energy manifestation called *Shen*. One very basic translation of Shen in English is "spirit". Shen should be comfortably housed (anchored) in the heart. This will provide a sense of calmness, inner peace, and a feeling of bliss. When Shen is not properly anchored due to any type of imbalance, it can result in the expression of anxiety. The individual will then feel an undercurrent of anxious energy. He/she may feel nervous without any apparent reason, and it feels to the individual as if they are not grounded.

A good term for this would be "free spirited," but not in the common Western meaning; rather, with the intention of a person whose spirit is not anchored and is constantly in the state of fluctuation and tension. As it was discussed in the case of liver and anger, this concept also works in both directions. Thus, if we have any type of heart pathology, we need to consider issues related to Shen disturbance, like anxiety. And anytime we are addressing issues related to anxiety and nervousness, the heart organ must be considered. In Chinese Medicine, many cases of insomnia are addressed by treating the heart to anchor the patients' Shen, which will calm them down and bring peaceful sleep.

Spleen >< Somber – Pensiveness - Worry

Based on Traditional Chinese Medicine, the spleen plays a great role in the metabolism of nutrients and energy within our bodies. There is a classic TCM condition called: "SP Qi Xu" or "*Spleen*

Energy Deficiency," which leads to sluggishness and fatigue in the patient's body. Until a few years ago, the spleen didn't have a specific physiological function in Western Medicine. It was regarded a "vague" organ with association to different systems (circulatory, lymphatic), but no clear function. The spleen's function in Western Medicine has been more defined in the last part of the 20th century, and it is now mostly regarded as an immune enhancer. From Western Medicine's perspective, the spleen has a role in the production of red blood cells and is one of the main organs involved in fighting against any disease. It removes old blood cells and holds a reserve of blood in case of hemorrhage. It also recycles iron and synthesizes antibodies through blood and lymphatic circulation.

From the Chinese Medical point of view, the physiological role of the spleen is closely related to the function of the adrenal glands and plays a great role in hormonal regulation and balance in our bodies. But for our discussion, it is the emotional energy of the spleen (referred to as pensiveness) that interests us. The feeling of introversion and depression, being quiet (or in some Chinese interpretations, being calm and quiet), results from the imbalance of spleen energy. I have to explain here that we are looking at a medical system which is closely connected to the Chinese culture and way of life. What Chinese people of two thousand years ago might have (culturally) interpreted as *pensiveness* can easily be related to what we in the West refer to as *depression.*

The connections between the emotion of worry (depression) and the spleen organ can also be linked to one of the adrenal gland functions. There is a condition called "adrenal fatigue" which manifests itself when the patient has a false sense of energy, but is also feeling an underlying tension and nervousness. The person may feel both physically and emotionally drained, and it feels as if the patient is running on empty.

Lung >< Grief – Sadness - Loss

The lungs behave like two massive filters in our bodies. Their massive surface area is in charge of a two part exchange between the external universe and the internal world (Lungs and Intestines are referred to in some ancient medical texts as the *internal skin*). These exchanges are very critical in the minute to minute physiological and energetic functions of our bodies. The first exchange introduces what's outside of our bodies to what's inside. (The air we breathe travels within and introduces external molecules to the inside of our bodies) The second exchange takes place outside of the lungs and at the cellular level when cells discard their waste, and receive nutrients and oxygen through the circulatory system. Although the lungs are not directly involved at the second level of exchange, they provide the necessary fuel for it to take place.

Lungs are the organs responsible for one of the most intimate connections between our bodies and the outside world. They are basically the first line of contact between anything we inhale and every living cell inside of our bodies. According to Al Lee and Don Campbell, authors of the book *"Perfect Breathing,"* 90% of the energy that our body uses comes directly from the breath, and 70% of the waste that is removed from the body is transported via the breath.

The manifestation of grief as an emotion is directly related to this organ from the Chinese medical stance. TCM believes that any type of chronic lung pathology can lead to this emotional imbalance and cause the patient to experience a sense of loss and longing. Thus anytime an individual is experiencing the loss of a loved one (or ending a long career by retirement or termination), they may also present with complications of their lung organ. Shortness of breath, asthma, emphysema, lung cancer, and anxiety attacks can all be manifestations of this type of Lung imbalance, depending on the individual's case presentation. One common expression to demonstrate this connection from the Chinese Medicine perspective is releasing deep sighs when we are sad and/or grieving.

Kidney >< Fear – Shock

Kidneys are very significant in both Eastern and Western medical systems as major regulators of fluids in our bodies. However in Western Medicine, each kidney is considered identical and a bilateral carbon copy of one another. But in Chinese Medicine, kidneys are considered to be different from side to side. The right kidney is considered the Yang kidney, and the left one represents Yin energy. Not only are they different energetically from the TCM view point, they also play a major role in the production of a substance called Jing. Jing can be defined as a primal substance responsible for keeping us young and vital. Jing is sometimes referred to as *"the essence of life within the body."* Some Chinese medical scholars even deem it identical to the concept of "genes" in the Western world. There are references from ancient Chinese medical text that Jing is produced from a fetus' kidneys and gives rise to all our organs and tissues. Interestingly enough, embryonic studies in the West also shows that the kidneys are usually the very first organ formed in a fetus.

Kidneys are also closely related to the emotion of fear (or a sense of shock) from the TCM point of view. That is not to be mistaken with timidity, since the gallbladder is the organ associated with that trait. Timidity is mostly associated with the lack of confidence and a sense of shyness. For this type of individual, making simple decisions can sometimes be a very long and difficult process since they might constantly doubt their own actions.

Primal fear is what we refer to when thinking of kidney deficiency. Individuals who are easily afraid of superstitions or the unknown (aliens, ghosts, the dark, etc.) are better representations of kidney imbalance. Again, since these relationships are always in both directions, it means individuals who were subjected to a horrifying experience or any type of natural disaster when young are more prone to have this type of kidney imbalance. One traditional association in TCM is the involuntary relief of the bladder (which we believe is due to weakness of the kidneys) in the case of shock from extreme fear.

Chapter Five

The Energy Network and Meridian System

In the previous chapters, I briefly discussed Dan Tians and explained their primary role as the three energy centers within the human body. We can now start to deepen our understanding of Dan Tians and also expand to the greater network of internal energy movements, or the Meridian System.

There are 14 primary meridians of Qi (energy) which cover the entire human anatomy from head to toe. Most of these meridians travel very close to the skin, but they also have an internal branch which connects to a specific internal organ. For example, the Liver Meridian travels alongside the torso and legs, however it also sends a branch to the liver organ. Therefore, these meridians can be used to treat the disease of the corresponding internal organ, or to treat the local issue on the superficial pathway of the meridian.

Example

By evaluating the lung meridian of the arm (Figure D), you can see that its external pathway starts on the chest and travels down the anterior aspect of the arm to the thumb. There are several points on this channel that can be used in the treatment of asthma, coughing, or shortness of breath (the lung organ.) The same points can also be utilized for the treatment of arthritis pain in the wrist, or tendonitis of the elbow (based on their anatomical locations.) The internal branch of any meridian which connects to a specific internal organ will manipulate and balance the energy of that organ (the lungs in the case of the Lung Meridian.)

LUNG *(Yin)*

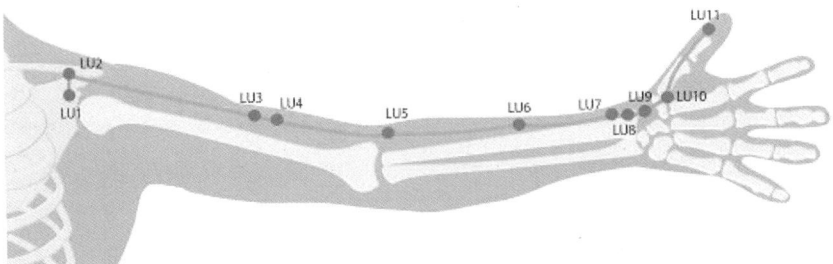

"Reprinted with Permission from - All-About-Acupuncture.com - All Rights Reserved."

Figure D

Acupuncture treatments utilize some of these specific "acupoints" on the targeted meridian to treat the disharmony within the related organ or the targeted meridian. When acupuncturists treat a patient for a specific imbalance, they intend to use "acupoints" to access and manipulate the Qi. The main goal is to encourage the body to return to its natural state of balance and find inner harmony (not in the poetic sense but the therapeutic one). The synergy which is created between several acupuncture points while stimulated with needles at the same time (and with the proper intention) will cause a healing response in the body. I always tell my patients that I (as an acupuncturist) am *not* the healer when it comes to their positive results from my treatments. I tell them that I only provide the tools for their body to create its own internal healing crises and to correct an imbalance; I am a facilitator of sorts.

The main concept of the *healer within* has become the driving force behind my need to write this book. Since I began realizing the awesome power of individuals and their body's ability to correct its imbalance, I started exploring ways to mimic the same effect without receiving an actual acupuncture treatment. I then created easy to apply methods based on the Traditional Chinese Medical understanding of emotional imbalance and its relationship to our internal organs. The main purpose of this book is to communicate with the general public (not just my own patients) the effective treatment of mild to moderate emotional ailments, using these easy-to-follow techniques. Emotional Energy Transformation will empower every individual to connect with their internal resources and enable them to start a private healing process. Personal awareness of one's body from the energetic perspective, and the internal energy movements within the body, becomes necessary to access this vast internal resource. My goal is to present you with easy to follow instructions to improve your understanding and increase your ability to transform your own internal energy.

There are many different views regarding our internal energy system. There are cultural differences between founding civilizations and technical differences within each culture. My personal interpretation comes from years of studying meditation, martial arts, practicing Qi Gong, and work/study as an acupuncturist. I believe that all the meridians cross through and are connected with our three Dan Tians (DT), or energy centers.

Imagine a vast fiber optic network of energy inside our bodies with three main hubs or *transformation and recycling and replenishing* centers. One is in the lower abdominal region, one is in the chest area, and one is in the area of our head. The Meridian Network travels inside our bodies and covers all the internal organs and tissues while connecting with our three Dan Tians. Every single cell is aware of and is affected by its quality, quantity, and movements. The more in touch we become with our bodies, the more intensely we are able to feel this network's existence and movements.

Chapter Six

Understanding the Dan Tian Energy System for Emotional Balance

All of the three energy centers are involved in transforming and transporting Qi (energy) in our bodies. They receive, regulate, and transform many different forms of energy on a daily basis. It is important to bear in mind that all three DTs are also connected to one another and influence each other's function. The entire energy system is a closed circuit (much like the cardio-vascular system) which is connected through the meridians and DTs within the body.

My belief is that our lower Dan Tian, which is located in our lower abdominal area, has a deeper connection with this planet and our natural surroundings. It is what keeps us connected (grounded) to earth and is a dynamic part of its biosphere. Lower Dan Tian is also more involved in the physiology of our bodies and maintaining its "physical" state of health. There are references about this Dan Tian "governing" (managing) all of the major organs residing within the abdominal cavity. [Aside from the heart and lungs, all other vital organs reside within the abdominal cavity. These two body cavities are separated by a thin layer of muscle called the diaphragm, which is also heavily involved in the act of breathing]

The second energy center (middle Dan Tian), which is located in the chest cavity, is much closer to the heart and lungs and more involved in our emotional health. It is responsible for managing the energy which we exchange with all other beings (human and animals) on this planet. It acts as a gatekeeper for most of the emotional energy exchange which takes place when we interact with others. The sense of comfort you might feel when meeting a loved one, or the sense of anxiety when entering a room full of strangers, are all received via this energetic conduit.

The third energy center (higher Dan Tian) is closely connected to the central nervous system and the vast (mostly unknown) processing capability of the brain. It brings us a sense of intellectual identity and supports all the mathematical analyses of the brain. The third Dan Tian is also involved in the relationship between us and what's above and beyond our planetary and physical realm.

Lower – Base – First Dan Tian

The lower DT is what keeps us physically balanced and centered, and it provides us with the sense of being grounded within our physical body. As I mentioned earlier, it is closely connected to all the internal organs within the abdominal cavity. It also governs and maintains our sexual energy, so it is important to pay close attention to this DT when working with issues regarding physical boundaries and/or past (negative) sexual experiences. It also plays a major role in regulating the creative energy rooted in the expression of one's sexuality. If you recall from earlier discussions, energy never dies, it only transforms. Thus most forms of art (music, poetry, painting, etc.) that are expressed by the artist stem from this DT via an internal transformation process. One example of such transformation can be observed in the massive collections of poetry created by 7th century Persian poets like Rumi and Hafiz surrounding love. There are scholars who argue that one of the main driving forces behind their fixation with symbolic references to love in their work is mostly the result of the sexually suppressed culture of their time.

The lower DT is located within our abdominal cavity, and is also what is referred to as the body's center of gravity. Its role is proximal to the health of our lower intestines, kidneys, and sexual organs. Many of the physiological and neurological processes which signal control, inhibition, and creation or design to our brain and central nervous system are related to this DT. It is responsible for the sense of being creative, yet centered within our actual physical boundaries. It is what's keeping us grounded and connected to the Earth.

The lower DT is the energetic base or powerhouse, not only for creative energy, but also for the actual physical distribution of energy within the body. This is what we refer to (even in Western culture) as "energy" when we are talking about our daily activities. For instance, when we feel fatigued and say, "I am running a little low on energy", or "I don't have much energy these days", we are actually referring to the energy of our lower DT. It is also one of the major components for transformation and distribution of the energy throughout the body. One major aspect of this kind of energy is to help move our muscles and provide a force to allow us to take part in routine daily activities.

Middle – Chest – Second Dan Tian

The Middle DT is mostly involved with regulating and managing our feelings and emotions. It is the first point of contact for all the emotional energy which enters our body, and it is how we connect with others emotionally. When you first meet a person and feel either comfortable or uncomfortable, it's through this gateway that their energy first enters your body. When you walk into a room and immediately feel nervous (or at ease), it is through this DT that you are experiencing that first initial feeling. It is closely related to the organs within the chest cavity (the heart and lungs), and that's why most cultures have many references concerning the heart's connection to one of the most intense human emotions: Love.

Unlike the other Dan Tians which are semi-vague and rather difficult for most Western cultures to grasp, the middle DT is pretty well known and easy to relate to for most Westerners. This DT is very important (and usually overactive) in the Western cultures, since people are more emotionally charged in their actions, and easily excited when they are exposed to raw emotional energy. Most of us who live in the West are usually more impulsive in our decision making process and react immediately to most emotional impulses. We usually react quickly to most external emotional stimuli, rather than letting it process and sink deeper in a calmer, internal environment. This DT, closely related to the function of our sympathetic and parasympathetic nervous systems, is therefore closely involved in the regulation of the biochemistry and the physiological aspect of our emotions. It is what I like to refer to as the emotional gateway for our bodies.

As mentioned previously, all feelings and emotions in relation to another being or a situation outside of our bodies are introduced through this DT. Unfortunately though, we usually capture and store this type of energy in our middle DT (which resides in the chest cavity) without processing it properly. In the long run, according to Chinese medical philosophy, this practice will cause disharmony and will lead to disease. Many cardiovascular and pulmonary issues can be related to stagnation of energy in this part of the body. Energy stagnation in the middle DT can cause anxiety disorder, which when bottled up will lead to a "panic attack", or what I like to call *emotional energy overload*. Medical conditions like heart palpitations, tachycardia, chest tightness or angina, shortness of breath, and asthma, without being related to a physical pathology (meaning that are *not* caused by a leaky heart valve, or actual physical blockage in an artery), can be successfully treated by addressing the stagnated energy in this area of the body.

A common issue which will result in the stagnation of energy in the middle Dan Tian is the lack or deficiency of active communication between this DT and the lower DT. In most cases, when we are exposed to an external source of emotional stimulation (which enters our body through this gateway), we either store it in the chest cavity, or have it ascend to our head for intellectual analysis. Storing "unprocessed" energy within the second DT can result in cardiovascular and pulmonary conditions when repeated over and over for a number of years. On the other hand, when this type of "unprocessed" energy has ascended to our head, it can cause an over-stimulation of our upper DT. Because this type of energy is not easy to process (it's not meant to be intellectually analyzed) for the upper DT, it creates energy stagnation which can lead to many physical dysfunctions. Conditions like migraine headaches, dizziness, tinnitus (chronic ringing in the ears), and sinus congestion are just a few that come to mind. However, the most prominent pathology which I see resulting from this phenomenon is what's referred to as *brain fogginess* and *lack of concentration*. This can easily lead to difficulty focusing in young adults and manifests via conditions like attention deficit disorder (ADD), and in some cases hyperactivity, or a constant low grade anxiety disorder. These conditions are usually diagnosed at a very young age, and are treated in most cases with psychostimulant drugs like Ritalin. Something that is usually puzzling to parents of these young patients is the sense of calmness and focus their children experience when put on drugs which, in essence, are speed. From my perspective, the drugs provide a temporary (false) burst of energy to the brain, to move through the cloud of all the stagnated energy in the upper DT, and a sense of focus, clarity, and control is produced while the patient is under its influence.

Upper – Higher – Third Dan Tian

The third and higher DT is closely related to our intellect, imagination, and creativity. Although a part of its function is related to our analytic and calculating mind (it aids in even our most ordinary brain functions), its main role is well beyond the brain as an organ. In Traditional Chinese Medicine, the brain is considered as just another organ with a physiological job to do. It is by far our most complex organ, but it is *not* our only residence of consciousness and awareness throughout the body. Our brain mainly functions as a neurological command center for all of our sensory experiences and our motor functions. However, like any other organ, it has a biological function and physiological purpose. There is a very close relationship between the neurological network and our third DT, but this is only one aspect of its complex and dynamic relationship with our bodies.

The function and purpose of our third DT extends well beyond the comprehension of day to day perceptions of what we refer to as "reality". This DT's location is obviously proximal to the main hub for our central nervous system, which is the brain. However, its function is not limited to the role of the brain as an organ in the regulation of our bodily functions. It is also meant to be related to the higher consciousness, and it acts as our source of connection to what's above and beyond our physical body. If the first DT governs the sense of self-awareness in relation to our natural surroundings and is the connection between us and this planet, and our second DT is the regulator of our emotions and the connection we have with other beings on this planet, then the third DT is our connection to what's above and beyond the physical realm, and what is explainable with our logic and the laws which govern this planet.

I would like to make a clarification that I am *not* referring to any "known" theories or debatable ideas (like aliens or ghosts), when I say what is beyond this physical world. The beauty of this realm resides within the mystery of its unknown.

The three energy centers work in conjunction with one another and the Meridian Systems, and this delicate network of information and energy plays a very important role in what creates the perception of our daily experience, life. From the energetic point of view, they are maintaining the life force which makes us sentient. They are also connected with one another to transform and transport energy internally via the meridian network, which is also used as places of Qi gathering, or recycling and transformation.

Every time we take a breath, energy flows inside our bodies and transforms through these energy centers. Everything we eat gets transformed energetically and distributed via our internal organs, which are affected and run by these energy centers. Our mental, emotional, and intellectual perceptions of every experience we go through in life are affected and influenced by these energy centers and their network of meridians. Thus, to have a healthy and balanced view of our existence, we need to have a better understanding of this network and connect with it at a deeper, yet more conscious, level.

Chapter Seven

I.

Breath-Work and Visualization

The most instantaneous way to connect to our internal energy is through our breath. Every breath we take is the representation of the life force, which enters the body and transforms into energy to keep us alive.

o   *Physiological Breathing*

From the physiological standpoint, there are two main exchanges that take place every time we breathe. The first exchange happens in the organ, the lungs, which primarily act as a large filter for air. The second exchange happens at the cellular level, when waste is traded for nutrients.

To explain in more detail:

The first exchange takes place in the gathering of specialized cells that form millions of tiny, exceptionally thin-walled air sacs called alveoli. Air enters into the body via the nose and the mouth and travels into the lungs through the trachea. It then finds its way down and through hundreds of branches to get to the last group of small cells (alveoli). These very small, but also very important, cells are surrounded by tiny blood vessels that receive oxygen and nutrients from the air we have taken in. The second exchange takes place at the cellular level when the nutrition rich blood reaches every single cell in our bodies to transport nutrients and receive waste via various types of osmosis.

This ongoing and ever present cycle happens with every breath we take. Physiologically, this process is the most essential component of being alive. We will cease to exist if it's not present even for a few short minutes.

o   *Energetic Breathing*

From the energetic standpoint, there are also cycles of movement and exchange which take place with every breath we take. The first level of exchange happens when we bring what's outside of the body inside. As we take in a deep breath, the energy of our surrounding environment (and the atmosphere) enters our bodies. This exchange of outside and inside energy causes a reaction that affects the entire body. Several factors can influence the quality of this exchange, and the level of transformation which it will cause. But the most important factor is our own level of awareness of this energy transformation. This is what is referred to in Zen practice as being connected to your surrounding nature, or *being present*.

The second level of exchange happens at our lower DT. In the same way that we exchange nutrients and waste physiologically through the lungs, we can exchange and transform energy through our DTs. The exchange and transformation happen within the Dan Tian system, and the energy gets transported via the meridian network system. This second phase can also be called the *"Dan Tian exchange"* or the *"Dan Tian breathing"*.

This practice is well known within all the different branches of Asian Martial Arts philosophies. It's one of the very first principles taught to a seeker of internal power, rather than the bulking up of external musculoskeletal strength. There is a very large community adhering to this style of practice, both inside and outside of China. In the West, it's mostly known as *Qi Gong* (working with energy). The awareness of this state is one of the most important aspects of any advanced energy work and practice.

This second phase of DT breathing has similarities with what's known as abdominal or diaphragmatic breathing, but it is not limited to our physical tissue and the physiological process of breathing. It is meant to reach beyond the physical aspects of breathing and the neurochemistry of oxygen and carbon dioxide exchange. The DT exchange is closely affected by one's level of energy awareness, and of its existence and movement within the body. The more in tune we are with our own energy, the easier it becomes to feel and benefit from its existence.

In advanced stages of most self-awareness practices like TM (Transcendental Meditation) or Zen Buddhist meditations, the participant's aim is to cultivate energy with every breath they inhale. The fact that we can consciously make small deposits of energy every time we take a breath is a very powerful concept. It is what gives the practice of DT breathing immense health benefits.

In upcoming chapters, you will learn techniques to become better connected to your own internal resources through a set of simple movements and easy breathing exercises. These techniques will create a unique sense of self-awareness and empowerment which can then be used later on to address minor or major health related issues.

Since many of us in the West have been encouraged from very early on in our childhood to place our health into the hands of capable medical personnel, a vast population has been disconnected from our own massive internal resources. However, these resources are omnipresent and universal to all human beings; therefore, it is easy and very natural to get better in touch with them and to enjoy the sense of internal power which they will create deep inside. Also, they will bring about preventative and curative health benefits that are almost unimaginable to most Western cultures.

II.

The Power of Visualization

When we look at something, the brain and the visual cortex normally translate the reflection of light which emits from that object. Every object has some universal and general qualities, which makes it easy for everyone to identify with it in reference. For instance, when we hear a story that someone was driving a car and ran into a tree, we view that tree like most other trees, with roots in the ground and trunks and branches reaching skyward. However, if we are personally present and are viewing the actual tree, then each individual tree has unique characteristics which makes it stand out to us differently. Those unique and individual characteristics like shape, size, color, and texture can even make the experience of viewing the same tree very diverse for different individuals based on their particular viewpoints.

Even the individual impressions that we take from being physically present and looking at an object can vary. Every time we look at an object, a flower for instance, we record a mental image of that flower deep in our brain. The image we record though depends on a wide variety of external and internal factors. These factors can be things like the lighting, or our viewing angle, or the feelings, or emotions that are affecting our internal mood at that moment. Whether the differentiating factors are imposed by our external environment, or caused by our own internal processes, they always influence the quality of our experience; thus the mental image we capture from that flower. We can then "see" the image of that same flower later, even when we are removed from the actual physical site, based on that mental recording data which exists within our brain. A mental picture has direct associations with reality for us only if we have already seen it. The image of the flower exists in our mind from the memory of our previous viewing.

The main difference between a memory and a vision then is that a memory consists of prerecorded events that are being replayed in our mind. A vision, on the other hand, is a completely brand new image which is *created* from a purely internal process. To most people, a vision is not normally linked with what we call "reality" since it has no memory associations. It is mostly created with what we like to call our *"imagination."* The definition of imagination is *to be able to form mental images*, and the default understanding of that ability is normally associated with fantasies. When someone says, "I have a vision" about something, it normally implies that they are making that vision in their mind before it might take place in their real life.

For instance, if you are planning to redecorate your house or your office, it is always better to start with a mental picture of your end result before moving in the first piece of furniture or painting any walls. When you create a mental image, you start your project (no matter how small or big) with a vision which will act as a compass. Although your vision may or may not be 100% in compliance with the end result, and you may modify it as you move along, it will provide you with a blueprint of what you are striving for.

I believe that simple example can easily describe the importance of visualization in the practice of energy awareness. Not only when it comes to home remodeling, but also to any other internal and transformational work. Having a clear vision is instrumental when we create something from scratch; however, it is just as crucial even when we wish to change or recreate an existing phenomenon. The same principle applies to our bodies and any physical, mental, or energetic transformation. When we practice guided visualization, or self- guided visualization, we create a vision about the internal changes that are taking place within our bodies. This practice is a very powerful tool in self-care and a great aid for any internal transformation from disharmony to health.

Chapter Eight
Connection, Cultivation, Utilization

I.

Connecting with Your Inner-Self (Your Own Energy)

The visualization exercise that I am about to describe is very easy to follow. You can start working on it at any location and in any situation; it's a very effective tool toward self-awareness and a deeper sense of inner connection. In the beginning, it will be beneficial to do this exercise in a quiet setting that is away from any distractions. However, after a short period of regular practice, you become deeply connected to your own inner energy, and the benefits of this exercise (along with many others that we will discuss in coming pages) can become instantaneously available to you under any circumstance.

The Connection Exercise

To make the following exercise easier to follow, I've broken it down into three sections:

1. Locating and visualizing your lower Dan Tian.
2. Connecting to your lower Dan Tian via your breath.
3. Anchoring your thoughts, grounding your body, and calming your mind.

Emotional Energy Transformation

Please consult with your treating practitioner if you have any health concerns or hesitations before starting any exercise regimen

Locating and Visualizing Your Lower Dan Tian

- Find a quiet place, take a deep breath, and relax...
    - You may close your eyes after reading different parts of the exercise for a few seconds to briefly visualize, and then move on to the next section.
- Start by visualizing your lower DT, or lower energy center
- I will provide you some easy to follow anatomical references to aid with locating and visualizing your lower DT:
    - On your abdomen, visualize a line which connects your navel to the top portion of your pubic bone.
    - Find the midsection of that line, and visualize it like a small dot on your abdomen (the size of a pea).
    - From that point (dot) on your abdomen, visualize a second line which is cross-sectional, starting to connect the front wall of your body, to the back wall of your body.
    - Now, find the midsection of the second line, inside your abdominal cavity.
- Start by visualizing a sphere, the size of an orange suspended in that location, inside your abdominal cavity.
- That general area is where I want you to visualize your lower DT, and to focus your attention, each time you take a breath.
- Visualize your DT as a condensed field of energy – just like the sun which is at the center of our solar system – with the same kind of intense white color (the color of light) and qualities. See it like a very condensed field of energy.

Connecting to YourLower Dan Tian via Your Breath

- Visualize your DT expanding (ever so slightly) every time you inhale, and shrinking (slightly) with every exhale.
- Now, start visualizing every breath you take like a wave of energy that is entering your body through your nose and your mouth.
- A helpful image to use when visualizing your breath as a wave of energy is to think about it like the steam escaping from a boiling tea pot and travelling in space.
- To make this more tangible, you can visualize the wave of energy (your breath) with some qualities, like a unique texture or color.
- Imagine that with every breath you take, a wave of energy enters your body and travels all the way down to merge with your lower energy center (DT).
- Visualize this phenomenon as if each breath travels or descends within your body all the way down to your lower DT; imagine you are making a small *deposit of energy* into your lower DT with every breath you take.

Anchoring Your Thoughts, Grounding Your Body, and Calming Your Mind

- Imagine that all your thoughts, regardless of their origin, are floating around in your head (your mind). They could be pleasant thoughts, or not so pleasant ones. They could be memories of the past, or worries about the future. You need to envision them collectively as simply your "thoughts". Now, free them of any individual emotional attachments you might have to a single "thought".
- You can get more creative with this process. You can envision your thoughts like floating images, numbers, letters, or sentences, with different fonts and colors, bouncing around in your head. You can view them as small clusters of energy,

with different shapes and sizes. They could have sound associations, or flashing images, or colors. The point is to visualize them all collectively, as your "thoughts" bouncing around in your head.

- Now, start visualizing them gravitating toward the wave of energy, which is cycling from your head, down to your lower DT, every time you take a breath.

- Visualize this process as if the wave of energy (your breath) is creating a downward force like a reverse whirlwind, or a vacuum, which is pulling down all the floating energy in your head (your thoughts), to your lower DT.

- Visualize your mind emptying all of your thoughts, with every descending wave of energy (your breath) that is travelling from your head to your lower DT.

- Concentrate on a very active and powerful descending movement of energy, traveling from your head, face, jaws, neck and throat, to your lower DT.

- You can also visualize this process like gradual opening of a sink or bathtub drain, and the rushing down of water, as your thoughts leave your mind.

- With every breath you take, you feel calmer and more deeply connected to your core. With every breath you take, you become more grounded and centered.

- You start experiencing the peace and quiet resulting from the emptiness of your mind. It is as if you have pushed the pause button and stopped *all* the ongoing internal conversation inside your mind. You have freed your mind to be calm, quiet, and in total peace. You are also centered and deeply grounded within your body and closely connected (present) to your surrounding environment.

- When you are finished with this exercise, slowly bring your attention back to the physical presence of your body. Feel refreshed and filled with vibrant healing energy which you have accessed from within your own body.

The aim of this simple exercise is to raise your awareness and to teach you how to become better connected with your inner self. It will turn your attention inward, rather than being preoccupied with what is taking place outside of your body. Plus, it will allow you to actually *feel* the energy present within, and relate to your own body from the energetic perspective. This is a very powerful first step toward internal energy awareness which will later lead to cultivation and utilization of your own energy.

As you get better at doing this exercise, you will be able to instantly connect with your lower DT by simply taking a deep breath. This connection will provide you with an immediate sense of calmness and inner control; it can take place under any circumstance. I use DT breathing exercises all the time and find them very helpful when I am tending to my patients and moving between different treatment rooms and need to turn my focus from one patient to another to be fully "present." I also use it to prepare for any type of engagement where I am speaking in front of a large audience. Like anything else in life, repetition will make you better and more efficient at this exercise.

II.
Cultivating Energy

As you become more in touch with your inner self, you can start cultivating (gathering) energy on a conscious level. The concept of energy cultivation is very different than adding to the actual physical amount of energy within the body. It is more like adding density and power, rather than the actual physical space. One thing we need to keep in mind when it comes to energy is it's not about the size and physical space, but rather the concentration and the power.

The process of energy cultivation begins when we are born; like breathing, it happens on an unconscious but continuous level. Imagine breathing all your life, but without ever taking a long, deep, refreshing breath. Learning about your internal energy transformation will allow you to take those long and deep energetic breaths, rather than just getting the minimum that's necessary to stay alive. It will enhance your productivity and focus, and it will also allow you to function at your optimum level.

To cultivate energy you need to use advanced visualization techniques. I always like to start with the "connecting" exercises of DT breathing and visualize a deep connection to my lower DT. It will automatically ground my body and focus my attention inward. Being in this state allows for our senses to work cohesively and activates the parasympathetic nervous system. We can then start from a very calm and collected place, and then add layers to deepen the benefits of the exercise. Colors can also play an important role in this stage of your practice.

Please consult with your treating practitioner if you are under care to treat any type of chronic conditions before you start with any exercise regimen

The Cultivation Exercise

- Always start by visualizing your lower DT, or lower energy center.
- Find and visualize your DT as a sphere the size of an orange, suspended within your abdominal cavity (this was discussed in an earlier "connection" exercise).
- Focus your attention on your lower DT each time you take a breath.
- Visualize it expanding ever so slightly with every inhalation you take.
- Visualize it shrinking slightly with every exhalation.
- Visualize it pulsating very gently, yet continuously, with the rhythm of your breath.
- Imagine that every breath you take enters your body like a wave of energy.
    - When I say a *wave of energy*, I am referring to what was discussed earlier during the "connection" exercise: a

wave that has some texture and amplifies the way that steam travels in space.

- Visualize this wave of energy with pale blue color, like a clear sky.
  - Please don't feel confined to my choices of colors for these exercises. You can certainly play with different colors and choose whatever works for you to focus your attention better.
- Visualize and follow as this wave of energy travels all the way down to merge with your lower energy center (DT).
- Visualize the moment when the blue colored wave merges with your DT and becomes more apparent as it seeps inside the bright white colored sphere.
- Now, visualize and follow every wave of energy (breath) as they travel within your body, and descend all the way to your lower DT to make a small deposit of energy from the outside world into your body.
- Visualize that every wave travels within your body to merge with your lower DT and instantly transforms to become one with the energy of your DT.
- **[EXIT PROCESS]**

    When you are finished with this exercise, slowly bring your attention back to the physical presence of your body. Feel refreshed and filled with vibrant healing energy which you have accessed from within your own body.

Just like the sun, which is a massive field of energy, our DTs are also fields of energy. And also like the sun, they will convert and transform everything that comes into contact with them. Please keep in mind that this process doesn't add to the actual "physical" size of your DT, rather to its concentration and power. As I mentioned earlier, this is a *natural process* which is already taking place inside of our bodies; however, this exercise will enable us to *enhance* its benefits.

III.
Utilization Through Expansion and Self-Care Practice

Now that we have discussed *connection* and *cultivation,* it is time to talk about *utilization* of the internal energy. There are numerous ways to access and use our own Qi (energy) from the Chinese medical point of view. In fact, the practice of acupuncture can be described as one of these different methods. From the Qi Gong (working with Qi) philosophy, when an acupuncturist inserts needles to specific acupuncture points, he/she provides tools to the patient's body for correcting its imbalance. The synergy which takes place within the body due to placement of acu-points will cause an internal healing reaction, which then brings the body back into balance.

The true "healer" in any acupuncture treatment is the patient. The acupuncturist only acts as a "facilitator" of sort for this healing reaction to take place. Of course, I am *not* trying to undermine an acupuncturist's role in helping patients get over their illnesses.

The medical practitioner needs to have the proper knowledge and insight to be able to employ a relevant treatment and enable the patient's body to cause a positive response. However, I am a firm believe that our patients have much greater power over their own Qi (energy).

Think about it: even from the Western medicine's point of view, the patients are the ones who *respond,* or *do not respond,* to any course of treatment. This is especially true when it comes to caring for and managing chronic illness. But it is very relevant even when Western medical practitioners perform surgery, or even in triage cases. They do what needs to be done from their perspective, and then wait and see how the patient *responds* to the treatment.

We have subscribed to the idea of doctors as healers beginning many years ago. I feel this concept has become more relevant within the past two hundred years with the surge of Western Medicine, which has truly produced miraculous results in the treatment of trauma and epidemic diseases. I am actually a firm believer in its relevancy to treat patients and to produce optimum health. However, regardless of the technique used to treat an individual, I would rather to place the emphasis more on the patient, rather than the person providing the care. I believe that true healing happens deep inside and is caused more as the result of an energetic shift from the patient's body, rather than subscribing to Western or Eastern medical techniques. An intelligent patient should be closely involved and be empowered when it comes to his or her own medical care and treatment outcomes. It is through this close involvement and sense of personal responsibility toward one's health and wellness that a true course of healing process begins.

All of the exercises discussed in my book will offer you the ability to start practicing self-healing and correct possible internal imbalances. As you create and foster a deeper connection with your own body's healing energy, you can then start to control and influence its intention. You can reduce its stagnation, promote its concentration, and rectify imbalances. You hone the ability to direct it into, or out of, different organs, body parts, and physiological systems. These practices will act as a tool providing you with the ability to actually self-treat ailments. They also enable you to manage and control your feelings and have better foresight into the emotional outcome of your actions. You can use them to treat simple conditions like a mild headache, or mild cramps from Pre-Menstrual Symptoms (PMS), or to treat more complex and even chronic conditions like Attention Deficit Hyperactivity Disorder (ADHD), anxiety induced asthmatic attacks, and many more. The value of what I am offering is enabling you with a greater understanding and deeper connection to your inner power. This virtue can be relevant under any circumstance, whether it is a mental, psychological, or physical challenge which you are facing in life.

Please consult with your treating practitioner if you are under care to treat any type of chronic conditions before you start with any exercise regimen

The Expansion Exercise

[Startup Steps]

- *Always start by visualizing your lower DT, or lower energy center.*

- *Find and visualize your DT as a sphere the size of an orange suspended within your abdominal cavity (this was discussed in the earlier "connection" exercise).*

- *Focus your attention on your lower DT each time you take a breath.*

- *Begin with the active connection to your lower DT by the way of your breath.*

- *Visualize your DT expanding ever so slightly, every time you inhale, and visualize it shrinking slightly with every exhalation.*

- *Visualize it pulsating very gently, yet continuously, with the rhythm of your breath.*

- Now start by visualizing its expansion rate slowly becoming greater than its reduction rate.

- Every time you inhale, it will expand to two times greater than the time before.

- Visualize it slowly expanding from the size of an orange or a tennis ball to a volleyball size, and then slowly to a basketball size, and a yoga ball size. Then slowly visualize it expanding with every breath you take to reach beyond the boundaries of your physical body.

- Eventually, visualize yourself encapsulated within this energy field which stemmed from within your lower DT.

- Visualize your body suspended in this sphere which is perhaps the size of a small car, and experience yourself floating in complete peace and quiet within this energy field.

- Visualize that you are completely removed from your surrounding environment, and regardless of what's happening outside of your body, you are experiencing total inner peace and your mind is completely quiet.

- Visualize your body as very light and floating, and your mind as very calm and empty of all your thoughts.

- Now visualize that all your cells "collectively" (regardless of their physiological makeup or physical location) are responding to the energy field which is surrounding your body.

- Visualize yourself in a healing environment within the capsule that was created from your own healing energy of the lower DT.

- Continue visualizing the sphere around you pulsating (very slightly) with every breath you take.

- In this isolated moment, visualize that all the cells within your body are communicating freely and are in total unison.

- Visualize that they are all working with one intention and toward the same goal of creating an internal healing environment.

- Visualize that any disharmony, lack of order or chaos is resolved, and your body is in a state of perfect balance and harmony.

- If you are aware of any physiological condition, try to pay extra attention to the pain or discomfort which it is causing, or to the area of your body that is affected.

- Visualize your entire body now working in harmony to correct the imbalance which has caused the discomfort and becoming free from its pain.

- Envision yourself suspended within this healing environment which you have created yourself, and hold this image for as long as it's comfortable, or at least 10 minutes.

- When you are ready, start by visualizing your DT slowly shrinking with a greater rate than its expansion, until it returns to its previous size and settles in your lower abdominal area.

- **[EXIT PROCESS]**

    When you are finished with this exercise, slowly bring your attention back to the physical presence of your body. Feel refreshed and filled with vibrant healing energy which you have accessed from within your own body.

IV.
Moving and Working with the Qi within the Body

For this next exercise, I would like to invite you to use your active imagination and visualize the inside of your own body. Imagine that you have the viewpoint of a small exploratory particle and have the ability to actually view what is inside your body. From this vantage point, envision the inside of your body with different colors as you go through the next exercise. Visualize that you are freely moving about within your own body, floating on a wave of energy which is travelling inside. Imagine this wave can move from organ to organ and explore every corner of your anatomy.

For instance, you can visualize that you are "riding" a wave of energy which is blue in color and is traveling from your head to your lower abdominal area, but from an internal vantage point (rather than visualizing your body from outside), and with translucent skin. The main advantage of using this type of visualization technique is that it will allow (and encourage) you to turn your focus *inward* and become more connected with what is inside, rather than being distracted by what is taking place on the outside.

My recommendation is to set aside a few minutes every day and practice any or all of these simple exercises in the order which they were discussed. Having a regular daily practice will enhance your living experience and also add to the quality (and even the quantity) of your life.

Please consult with your treating practitioner if you are under care to treat any type of chronic conditions before you start with any exercise regimen

The Self-Scan/Checkup Exercise

[Startup Steps]

- *Always start by visualizing your lower DT, or lower energy center.*
- *Find and visualize your DT as a sphere the size of an orange suspended within your abdominal cavity (this was discussed in the earlier "connection" exercise).*
- *Focus your attention on your lower DT each time you take a breath.*
- *Begin with the active connection to your lower DT by the way of your breath.*
- *Visualize your DT expanding ever so slightly, every time you inhale, and visualize it shrinking slightly with every exhalation.*
- *Visualize it pulsating very gently, yet continuously, with the rhythm of your breath.*
- Now start visualizing your breath as it travels within your body like a wave of energy, and as if you are traveling and moving with this wave.
- Visualize the wave as it is entering and connecting with your lungs.
- Visualize that this wave of energy is not only entering your lung organ, but also surrounding it, slowly enveloping the entire organ.
- Now visualize that it is cleansing and repairing, removing any possible toxins and harmonizing your lungs to balance with the rest of your body.

- Now visualize and follow this wave of energy as it travels to enter and surround your heart organ.
- Visualize it massaging your heart muscle and moving from chamber to chamber to revitalize and energize your heart.
- Visualize that it is harmonizing your heart to balance with the rest of your body.
- Follow the wave as it's moving from your chest cavity to enter your abdominal cavity.
- Visualize the wave of energy entering your liver, which is sitting under your ribs on the right upper corner of your abdominal cavity.
- Visualize your liver as a large triangular shaped filter with small chambers which your blood is moving through.
- Now visualize that the wave of energy is cleansing and repairing your liver as it's moving in and around this organ.
- Imagine that the energy wave is harmonizing your liver to balance with the rest of your body.
- Right behind your liver sits a small pouch called the Gallbladder (GB). Its job is to store the bile which is produced by your liver and then eject it at the right time and with the right amount to your small intestine, which will aid with digestion of your food.
- Imagine that the wave of energy which you are traveling upon is massaging and revitalizing your GB.
- Envision that all toxins and possible stones are being removed and resolved as the wave of energy is entering and surrounding your GB.
- Imagine that it is harmonizing your GB to balance with the rest of your body.
- Now follow the wave as its making its way to the right side of your abdominal cavity to enter your stomach.

- Visualize it moving through your stomach and massaging its soft muscles, and going through all of the small pores which are responsible for secretion of digestive enzymes to aid your digestion.
- Visualize the wave is cleansing and rejuvenating your stomach and harmonizing it to balance with the rest of your body.
- Behind your stomach sits your spleen. Imagine that the wave of energy is also entering and surrounding your spleen.
- Spleen is a very important organ for our immune system and also a digestion aid (according to Chinese Medicine).
- Visualize your spleen as it's being treated by the wave of energy which is moving in and around it, and imagine that it is ridding it of all impurities or ailments.
- Visualize the wave of energy as harmonizing your spleen to balance with the rest of your body.
- Continue to follow the wave as it is entering your intestines.
- Visualize it moving within and around your small intestine and descending to your large intestine.
- Visualize the wave of energy cleansing and rejuvenating your intestines and harmonizing them to balance with the rest of your body.
- Now follow the wave as it is moving to enter and surround your kidneys, from the right kidney to the left one, and back and forth.
- Kidneys are another filter that are constantly dealing with impurities and also manage our bodily fluids. Imagine that the wave of energy is purifying your kidneys and cleansing them.
- Visualize the wave is cleansing and rejuvenating your kidneys and harmonizing them to balance with the rest of your body.
- Now visualize that this wave which you have maneuvered and followed throughout all your vital organs is moving to merge with your lower DT.

Emotional Energy Transformation

- Remember that your DT's job is to transform whatever energy that comes into contact with it into its own.
    o Remind yourself of the earlier analogy between the sun and your lower DT as a field of energy that instantaneously transforms or converts anything which comes in to contact with it into its own energy.
- Feel and envision your lower DT as it's receiving the wave of energy which has cleansed and harmonized your organs and as it is transforming it to its own energy.
- Imagine that you have not only cleansed and harmonized your entire body, but that you have also made a deposit of energy into your lower DT.
- **[EXIT PROCESS]**

    When you are finished with this exercise, slowly bring your attention back to the physical presence of your body. Feel refreshed and filled with vibrant healing energy which you have accessed from within your own body.

This is a *very* powerful and effective exercise if done on a regular basis. It may seem to take a long time when you first start practicing it, but after a few short sessions it will only take you a few minutes from start to finish. This exercise is like a *system check* that you can run through your body. We spend so much time tending to our outside appearances and our physical looks without giving much consideration to all the vital and important organs and body parts inside. By simply diverting our attention from outside to inside, just for a few short minutes, you can achieve a much deeper sense of inner harmony and feel more in balance.

Utilizing our own awesome power of self-healing and accessing our internal resources may appear unconventional in the eye of the "scientific, research-oriented" Western mind. But there is now increasing scientific evidence coming from numerous studies around what's called "mind/body" exercises which supports the amazing healing benefits of quieting the mind and focusing on the body. Dr. Robert Schneider, MD is the dean of the College of Medicine at the Maharishi University of Management in Fairfield, Iowa. He is also director of the university's government-sponsored Center for Natural Medicine and Prevention, one of sixteen such centers in the US. He claims that in the past few decades, there have been about six hundred studies worldwide on the positive effects of meditation (not medication) in regards to treatment of HTN (high blood pressure). These are mostly done with participants practicing a very simple and popular form of meditation called Transcendental Meditation I.

I know that in Western cultures, it's customary to be detail oriented and study every phenomenon differently, allowing the observer the advantage of objective comparisons. However (without trying to take credit away from any single study), I would actually like to propose a more Eastern and holistic view when it comes to all self-healing, and what is often referred to in the US as "mind/body" practices. I believe the most powerful aspect of all these types of healing exercises, or even things like regular prayer practices, is to simply divert the attention of the individual from the outside world to what is inside.

Being alive is a very dynamic physiological state which requires a heightened awareness of the physical body in the time space continuum. Our physical body is constantly repairing and rebuilding itself on a very active and ongoing base. At any given moment, there are millions of reactions and transformations which take place within our *internal cellular universe*. There have been references made to the relationship between the inside of the body and the outside universe from many ancient cultures spanning many centuries. Mystic philosophies like Sufism use the same metaphor to describe the vastness, order, and endless possibilities of both these internal and external worlds.

Another example to demonstrate such connection is the Yin/Yang symbol which was created centuries ago by the Chinese.

Emotional Energy Transformation

This symbol is used to represent perfect balance between the main two elements (or manifestations) of Qi which form the human body and, actually, the entire universe. The dark portion represents the Yin energy, and the light portion, the Yang. However, a small part of each element (the dark and light dots) is placed within the other to represent a snapshot of perfect balance and harmony. According to the Chinese, this represents a natural state which we all strive to attain in order to feel balanced inside, and also in harmony with the outside world. There are numerous cross references between the human body's internal universe and the universe outside of the human body. Ultimately, we are all different manifestations of the same energy which has formed (created) all there is and is present within everything. There are many books written about this symbol and its deeper meanings, and it's *not* the intention of this book to describe the "meaning" of the Yin/Yang symbol. I am making a reference to it simply because it reminds me so much of some pictures I have seen taken by the Hubble telescope from distant galaxies.

Courtesy of Nasa (www.hubblesite.org)

Just imagine that the Yin/Yang symbol, created by humans many centuries ago, is spinning around its axis at great speed. To me, the similarities between this centuries-old image and recent pictures taken by a super-telescope are hard to dismiss.

It is important to keep in mind that these observations took place centuries ago, and the ideas surrounding these philosophies stemmed without having access to all the technological advancements of the last few decades. I have to believe that somehow, at a very deep level, the wise men and women of the past who were making these observations and talking about these connections between the internal and external universe had an intuitive wisdom which lead them to make such claims. They probably felt these connections between the internal and the external universes, and that sense of deep connection provided them with greater insight about its manifestation.

I sometimes tell my patients who are struggling with debilitating diseases about these ideas. I believe that the same force which maintains balance throughout the vast external universe is also present within each and every one of us. We can feel its presence more strongly when we quiet our analyzing mind and become more in tune with the body's internal rhythm.

My intention is to remind us all of the existence of such connections, and to expand on the simple and natural state of internal peace and bliss to aid self-healing. Through these simple yet effective exercises, we can start cultivating a deeper connection with our own internal energy and utilize its awesome powers to excel in all levels.

V.
Self-Healing through Your Own Energy

The next group of exercises has proven to be very useful in treating almost any acute or chronic and long lasting ailments. Their main premise is to simply utilize your own healing energy to basically *"heal thyself."* However, it is important to note that these exercises are far more effective *after* you have learned about, and created a deeper connection with, your own internal energy via the previous exercises.

I started by teaching basic connection and cultivation exercises before I get any deeper into utilizing your own energy because I believe you need to know your energy and feel it first before you can actually use it. This principle is true in most aspects of life. We usually need to make an investment before we can start to withdraw. Therefore, I strongly recommend you follow the order of my teachings and start by practicing the first basic connection and checkup exercises for a while before you *graduate* yourself into more advanced levels. The same way that you need to train physically and mentally with shorter runs to be able to run a marathon, you need to practice energy awareness and create a deeper connection before you can control and utilize your own energy.

In the same way that you might suffer injuries and hurt yourself running a marathon without any prior training, you can potentially hurt yourself if you don't invest enough time in working on the early stages of cultivating Qi before making attempts to use it at deeper levels. You will simply be more effective at utilizing the more advanced exercises when you have a deeper sense of connection with your Qi before starting to practice them.

The following exercises can be used to treat any physical and physiological challenge that you are dealing with. They are not limited to any one condition or ailment. But to give you some perspective, I have used them effectively (both personally and for many of my patients) to treat acute conditions like: migraine headaches, sinus congestion, neck and shoulder pain, and faster healing of wounds and broken bones. I have also used these to help with patients who are suffering from more chronic conditions such as cancer patients undergoing chemotherapy (or natural) cancer treatments, irritable bowel syndrome, ulcerative colitis and/or Crohn's disease, chronic back pain, etc.

The following order of Self healing 1.0, 2.0, and 3.0 that I use to present these exercises is simply to demonstrate different levels of modification to utilize the same basic exercise and to treat different levels of imbalances present in the body.

Please consult with your treating practitioner if you are under care to treat any type of chronic conditions before you start with any exercise regimen

Self healing, 1.0

[Startup Steps]

- *Always start by visualizing your lower DT, or lower energy center.*

- *Find and visualize your DT as a sphere the size of an orange suspended within your abdominal cavity (this was discussed in the earlier "connection" exercise).*

- *Focus your attention on your lower DT each time you take a breath.*

- *Begin with the active connection to your lower DT by the way of your breath.*

- *Visualize your DT expanding ever so slightly, every time you inhale, and visualize it shrinking slightly with every exhalation.*

- *Visualize it pulsating very gently, yet continuously, with the rhythm of your breath.*

- Now start to visualize the movement of Qi within your body and through all the energy meridians.
  - Don't be concerned with too many details of specific meridians for this exercise, and just focus on a general sense of Qi moving within your body. It always helps me to envision this like fiber optic translucent lines, moving across my extremities and torso, with deep connections to all three DTs and all the vital internal organs. You can use colors to make this image more tangible for yourself.
- Imagine the energy network is moving the Qi at different speeds and in different parts of your body. And visualize that its movements are effected by your breath.
- Visualize that energy is moving from different parts of your body towards your DTs, and from your DTs back to different body parts.
- Now start to deepen your focus and concentrate on one of these waves as it's stemming from your lower DT. Visualize this wave with a distinctive color of bright white (like the color of light) which is extending from your lower DT.
- Now start visualizing a detailed sense of *control* over this energy wave, as if you can maneuver and guide it to any internal location and body part of your choosing.
- Visualize this wave is staying connected to your lower DT, and it is "extending" to reach and access wherever you wish for it to go throughout the body.
- Start by guiding and moving this extending wave of energy to the area of your body that is experiencing imbalance and needs attention.
- Visualize that this wave is reaching the desired organ, or tissue, or body part, and is slowly engulfing it with its energy.
- Visualize that your lower DT's source (healing) energy is now being directed to the area of attention as if it's being slowly *pumped* into that area.

- Keep this image for several minutes as you visualize that your DT is sending pure healing energy to that area of your body.
- You can hold this image for as long as comfortable, or about 5 minutes.
- When you are ready, start by visualizing the extending wave slowly returning to your lower DT.
- [EXIT PROCESS]

    When you are finished with this exercise, slowly bring your attention back to the physical presence of your body. Feel refreshed and filled with vibrant healing energy which you have accessed from within your own body.

Please consult with your treating practitioner if you are under care to treat any type of chronic conditions before you start with any exercise regimen

Self healing, 2.0

[Startup Steps]

- *Always start by visualizing your lower DT, or lower energy center.*
- *Find and visualize your DT as a sphere the size of an orange suspended within your abdominal cavity (this was discussed in the earlier "connection" exercise).*
- *Focus your attention on your lower DT each time you take a breath.*
- *Begin with the active connection to your lower DT by the way of your breath.*
- *Visualize your DT expanding ever so slightly, every time you inhale and visualize it shrinking slightly with every exhalation.*

Emotional Energy Transformation

- ***Visualize it pulsating very gently, yet continuously, with the rhythm of your breath.***

- Now start visualizing any body part or organ that is causing pain or disharmony within your body.
    - This exercise is very beneficial when dealing with an *acute* problem, such as an aching knee from running too long or a painful wrist from over-using the computer keyboard. Regardless of the cause of your condition, you can practice this simple exercise to aid your body with its healing benefits.

- Visualize that harmful (negative) energy is gathered in excess, and it is surrounding the affected area of your body (in Chinese medical terminology, this phenomenon is called Qi stagnation, or stasis of energy in one area).

- Visualize this stagnated energy, like a dark red or purple cloud, surrounding the affected area of your body.

- Visualize that the cloud of stagnated energy surrounding your ailing body part is slowly being transported to your lower DT via the meridians network.
    - As discussed earlier, there are pathways of energy travelling all around your body, and they branch out to cover your entire anatomy. You don't need to complicate this practice by trying to find and focus on a specific meridian. Just visualize that the stagnated energy is moving away from the effected organ and toward your lower DT like a wave of energy.

- Visualize that the dark red/purple colored cloud of Qi stagnation is gradually dispersing as it's moving toward you lower energy center.

- Visualize that the stagnated energy from the effected body part or organ is now merging with the energy of lower DT.

- Visualize the red color of this energy as it is seeping slowly inside of the bright white colored lower DT as if a cloud of ink is being released under water.
- Visualize the effected body part as healthy and free from the cloud of stagnated energy which was surrounding it.
- As discussed earlier, your lower DT is capable of transforming whatever energy it comes into contact with to its own source energy. Thus, visualize that not only is your organ now completely free of stagnated Qi, but your lower DT also has received a deposit of energy.
- **[EXIT PROCESS]**

    When you are finished with this exercise, slowly bring your attention back to the physical presence of your body. Feel refreshed and filled with vibrant healing energy which you have accessed from within your own body.

Please keep in mind that the function of your lower DT is to transform energy. Just like some other organs within the body (lungs, liver, kidneys) that function as filters, your DT can also act as a powerhouse for energy transformation. The main task of the mentioned organs is to receive unfiltered material and transform it into usable by-products for your tissues. And similarly, one of the main functions of your DT is also to filter unsuitable energy and transform it into a suitable form. Remember that your lower DT shares the same qualities with the largest star in our own solar system, the sun. The same way that whatever comes into contact with the sun instantaneously transforms to become one with its awesome energy, your DT is also capable of such a transformation of energy on a much smaller scale within your body.

Please consult with your treating practitioner if you are under care to treat any type of chronic conditions before you start with any exercise regimen

Self healing, 3.0

[Startup Steps]

- *Always start by visualizing your lower DT, or lower energy center.*
- *Find and visualize your DT as a sphere the size of an orange suspended within your abdominal cavity (this was discussed in the earlier "connection" exercise).*
- *Focus your attention on your lower DT each time you take a breath.*
- *Begin with the active connection to your lower DT by the way of your breath.*
- *Visualize your DT expanding ever so slightly, every time you inhale, and visualize it shrinking slightly with every exhalation.*
- *Visualize it pulsating very gently, yet continuously, with the rhythm of your breath.*

- Now start visualizing any body parts or organs which are causing pain or disharmony within your body.
    - This is a very beneficial exercise when dealing with both acute and chronic illness. It is primarily used for treatment of debilitating conditions like IBS (Irritable Bowel Syndrome), arthritis, or even cancer. Regardless of the cause of your condition, you can practice this simple exercise to aid your body with its healing benefits.
- Start visualizing that a line of energy is extending out of your lower DT to reach the affected area of your body.

- Visualize this wave of energy as it is travelling within your body as being bright white, the color of light.
- Now visualize that it reaches the desired area within your body and creates a bridge, a conduit of sort, between that area and your lower DT.
- Start visualizing that the energy is actively extending out of your lower DT to surround and enter every cell in and around the affected area of your body.
- Visualize that your own internal healing energy is stemming from your DT to gather around and saturate the affected area of your body, as if the targeted area of your body is floating, swimming, within the pool of white light which has stemmed from your lower DT.
- Visualize that every single cell, every single molecule, and every single atom within that part of your body is now being effected by the energy of your lower DT.
- Visualize your own healing energy as it penetrates and seeps into the deepest levels of every fiber of your being, and imagine that it is transforming your body to health.
- Visualize that it's balancing any imbalances, purifying any impurities, detoxifying any toxins, and is tonifying to revitalize your tissue to health.
- Now start visualizing a line of imbalanced (diseased) energy, releasing from the effected organ or body part to your lower DT, through the energetic bridge made between the lower DT and this area of your body.
- Keep this connection strong; continue to *see* that toxins and impurities are being released from your tissue to your DT, and that your tissue is being nourished by the energy of your DT, all at the same moment.
- Visualize that your body part is cleansing simultaneously, as your body is being nurtured, by your lower DT, through a *two-way* energy connection.
    - You can use colors to make this exercise more tangible.

Emotional Energy Transformation

- Keep the image of this active connection between your DT and the body part for at least 5 minutes (or as long as it's comfortable).

- Visualize that the wave of energy is slowly returning to reside within your lower DT, as it has rejuvenated and healed the area of concern within your body.

- **[EXIT PROCESS]**

When you are finished with this exercise, slowly bring your attention back to the physical presence of your body. Feel refreshed and filled with vibrant healing energy which you have accessed from within your own body.

Chapter Nine

Exercises for Specific Feelings and/or Individual Organs

There are two main cavities within the torso which contain most of our vital organs. The design is such that the two main organs which are in charge of pulmonary and cardiovascular systems (lungs and heart) are inside of the chest cavity and are closer to our head. The rest of the organs reside within the abdominal cavity, which is separated by a thin sheet of muscle called the diaphragm. And if you recall from our earlier discussions based on the Chinese medical model, many of the internal organs are associated with a set of feelings and have emotional manifestations. We are now going to explore practical ways for understanding and utilizing these emotional relationships from the energetic component. As we get to know ourselves and our bodies from this energetic point of view, we can understand and manage our emotions better.

Please keep in mind that all these recommendations and exercises are very effective *only* if they are done on a *regular* basis. Our bodies are magnificent in their ability to adapt, repair, and rebuild. However, most permanent changes happen gradually. Most smokers probably recall the first few times they smoked a cigarette. It is not natural for our lungs to inhale smoke; thus, we usually cough violently when first exposed to cigarette smoke. It will take several forceful inhalations and a few days before our bodies *adjust* to accommodate the unnatural behavior of inhaling smoke. However, the body adjusts and it will continue to adapt for as long as we smoke. Physiologically, the body adjusts by providing more blood and fluids to the lung tissue. It regulates our blood pressure and obliges itself to transform by creating a host of many other anomalies. The body is so very efficient at accommodating us that we can hardly feel any difference for a number of years, until the excess smoking catches up with, and exceeds, our natural repairing capabilities. In fact, if a person is in great health and smokes one cigarette, their body could *probably* repair all the damage from that in few hours. The same phenomenon is true for almost any human behavior when it's done in excess. Our bodies need to accommodate for all the extra calories we intake, thus it usually takes a while before the extra weight appears, and even more time before the extra cholesterol manifests itself, and more time before our arteries clog, etc.

The same principle then applies to the body when it is transforming back to health. The same way that the body adjusts to accommodate for our bad behavior, it will also transform to reward us for our good behavior. The lung tissue will immediately start to repair the damages from smoke inhalation, and the gastrointestinal system is constantly working hard to repair and replace unhealthy tissue, and it's thriving for stasis. It is the body's natural state to be healthy and balanced. All the exercises discussed in this book will strongly facilitate this transformation to health.

The point is that our bodies are magnificent at adapting to whatever behavior and lifestyle we choose. It's only a matter of time before it can make the proper adjustments to accommodate our behavior. Of course, elements like genetics and the environment can also play important roles in the speed of this process. However, given enough time, it's only through regular practice in which the body makes gradual, yet permanent, transformations. Although most recommendations and exercises discussed in this book are simple and easy to follow (with enough time and dedication), they will transform your body and provide the right environment for your natural healing abilities to be more effective.

LUNG *(Yin)*
LARGE INTESTINE *(Yang)*
EMOTIONAL CONNECTION *(Grief /Sadness)*

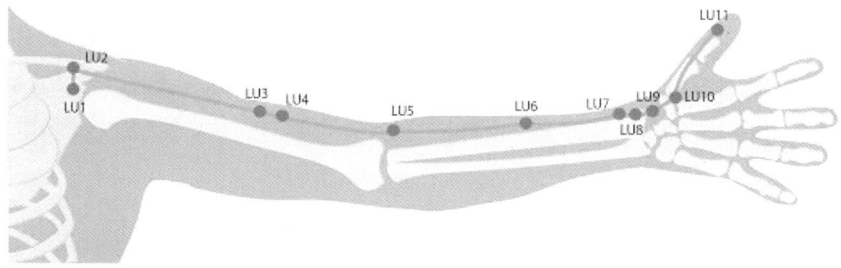

"Reprinted with Permission from - All-About-Acupuncture.com - All Rights Reserved."

Sadness and grief are the emotions related to our lungs. According to Traditional Chinese medicine, that is why we sigh when we are sad or depressed, and especially when we are grieving. A sigh is a forceful exhale; from the energetic perspective, it is a natural practice to reduce the heavy weight of the emotional burden residing within our chest cavity. What I encourage many of my patients to do when they feel sad or depressed is to practice active breathing with concentration on their exhalation.

The following exercise is designed to address the lung organ and its corresponding emotion.

The Lungs Exercise

[Disclaimer]

As discussed in earlier chapters, you don't need to have any medical conditions to start using any of the exercises recommended in this book. You can practice them preventatively (in fact that's especially what I hope for), if you feel energetically more vulnerable, in relation to a specific organ or body part. For example, practice the exercises preventatively if you have a family history of any type of cancers related to the organ or body part, or if you partake in the type of lifestyle which might be putting that organ or body part at a greater risk.

Emotional Energy Transformation

Please consult with your treating practitioner if you are under care to treat any type of chronic conditions before you start with any exercise regimen

Here is a list of *some* of the conditions corresponding to this exercise:

- Shortness of breath, asthma, bronchitis, chronic cough, upper respiratory infections (common cold), or other respiratory conditions.
- Sadness caused by grief or sense of loss.
- The desire to break the smoking habit.

- **[Grounding Process]**
- *Find a quiet place and plant your feet firmly on the ground.*
- *It is not necessary, but it can be very beneficial to do this exercise outside in the open air.*
- *Stand with your feet shoulder-width apart and your knees slightly bent.*
- *Relax your shoulders and neck, and rest your hands on your lower DT, and hold what's known as "the modified tree pose" (You can also do all of these exercises in a sitting position as well, as long as you are sitting on the edge of a firm chair with no armrests).*

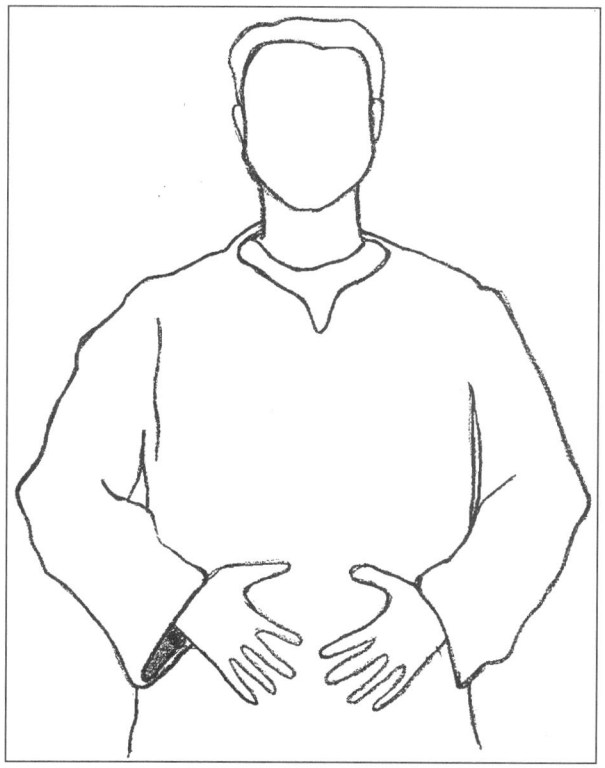

Modified Tree Pose (Lung Exercise)

- Start with an inhale while raising your arms slowly (elbows are straight, but not locked) in front of your body, and raise your hands above your head.

Emotional Energy Transformation

Arms elevated anterior (Lung Exercise)

- Your palms are open and facing forward.

- Finish your inhalation and hold your breath in this position just for a few, comfortable seconds (no more than 10 sec.) as you extend your chest to open your lungs, heart, and the middle DT.

- Then drop your arms down in front of your body, as you exhale forcefully (as if you were under water and paddling your body forward with both arms.)

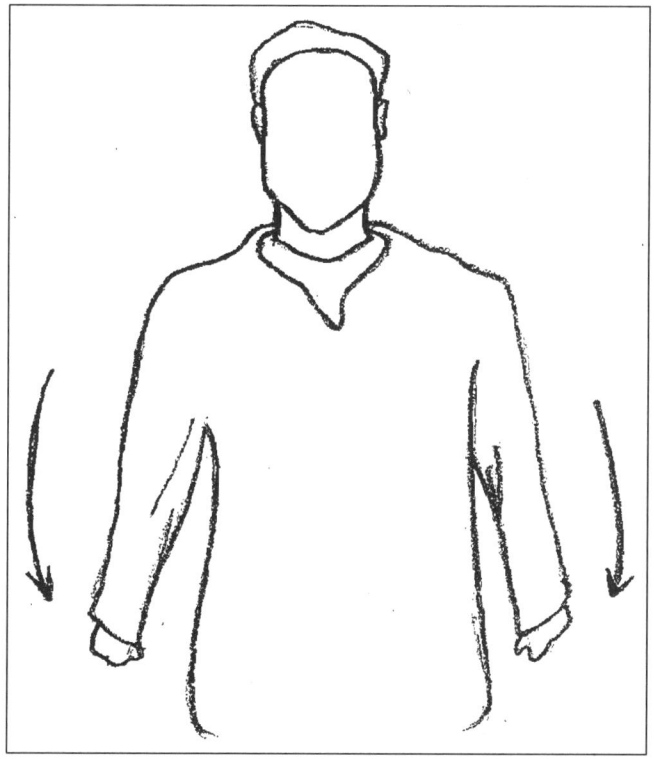

Drop both arms (Lung Exercise)

- Relax your face and shoulders as you drop down your arms and finish your forceful exhalation.
    - It will be more beneficial to make a loud noise as you exhale and drop down your arms. Your inhale should be slow and long, but your exhale should be brief and forceful.

Emotional Energy Transformation

- Let your hands naturally *bounce* back to your lower abdominal area (or just place them there), and start from the modified tree pose with an inhale.

Modified Tree Pose (Lung Exercise)

- Repeat this exercise 10 times, with the intention of letting the stagnated energy in your chest and lungs (exit), as you exhale to let go.

- **[EXIT PROCESS]**

    When you are finished with this exercise, slowly bring your attention back to the physical presence of your body. Feel refreshed and filled with vibrant healing energy which you have accessed from within your own body.

This simple exercise produces several different outcomes. It forces your body to actively move the stagnated air and energy, and it encourages deeper inhalations which will provide you with greater oxygen intake and thus better physiological functions. That alone will reduce the heavy and sluggish sensations and will provide you with more energy in a matter of minutes. Plus, it will physically eliminate toxins and cleanse not just your lungs, but your entire body, more rapidly. As you are exhaling forcefully, visualize that your lungs are emptying and you are chest is feeling *lighter*. The energy meridians for lungs are located bilaterally on the medial aspect of your arms and the anterior (front) portion of your upper chest area. With this exercise, you are also stimulating them to move the stagnated energy and help to clear your lungs.

I recommend this exercise to many of my patients who are trying to stop smoking. Not only does it clear their lungs faster and provide rapid detoxification, but it also helps them with the sense of grief they have from losing their long time companions, cigarettes.

Emotional Energy Transformation

HEART *(YIN)*
SMALL INTESTINE *(Yang)*
EMOTIONAL CONNECTION *(Panic / High Anxiety)*

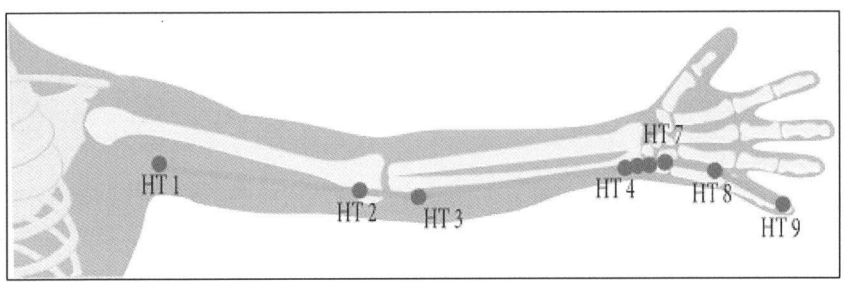

"Reprinted with Permission from - All-About-Acupuncture.com - All Rights Reserved."

From the Chinese medical perspective, the emotions which are related to this organ are excess joy, or excitement. However, the imbalance of the HT's energy will lead to what I believe is known in our culture as anxiety. We are having more and more people diagnosed with anxiety disorders and/or panic attack disorders in the United States. According to the National Institute of Mental Health (NIMH), approximately 40 million American adults ages 18 and older have issues with anxiety disorder in every given year. This is a staggering and, unfortunately, increasing number, and it is a major cause of many social issues and anti-social behavior in this country. Many teenagers and young adults are just simply less comfortable with communicating face to face, and prefer to rely heavily on texting, chat, or tweeting. Social anxiety is one of the major causes for the rise of Internet-based social networks.

In most cases, anxiety is caused by an over-exited sympathetic nervous system. There are major connections to sympathetic and parasympathetic nervous systems in our chest cavity and around the heart. By connecting to your middle DT and chest area consciously, and by visualizing your heart slowing its rhythm in your chest to beat calmly, you can stop an anxiety episode from ever turning into a full blown panic attack. This very simple exercise can dramatically reduce the severity of, or in many cases eliminate, anxiety.

The Heart Exercise

[Disclaimer]

As discussed in earlier chapters, you don't need to have any medical conditions to start using any of the exercises recommended in this book. You can practice them preventatively (in fact that's especially what I hope for), if you feel energetically more vulnerable, in relation to a specific organ or body part. For example, practice the exercises preventatively if you have a family history of any type of cancers related to the organ or body part, or if you partake in the type of lifestyle which might be putting that organ or body part at a greater risk.

Please consult with your treating practitioner if you are under care to treat any type of chronic conditions before you start any exercise regimen

Here is a list of *some* of the conditions corresponding to this exercise:

- Anxiety, panic attacks, ADD or ADHD.
- Shortness of breath, chest tightness, heart palpitation.
- Insomnia.

- **[Grounding Process]**
- *Find a quiet place and plant your feet firmly on the ground.*
- *Stand with your feet shoulder-width apart and your knees slightly bent.*
- *Relax your shoulders and neck, and rest your hands on your lower DT, and hold what's known as "the modified tree pose" (You can also do all of these exercises in a sitting position as well, as long as you are sitting on the edge of a firm chair with no armrests).*
- Start by taking deep, yet slow, and rhythmic inhalations, as you slowly extend your arms on the sides of your body, and visualize your chest opening up.

Emotional Energy Transformation

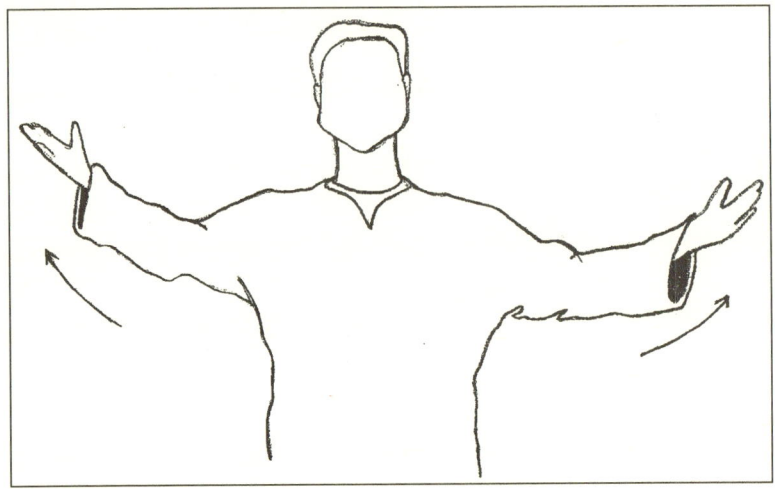

Raising arms (Heart Exercise)

- You need to hold your arms on either side of your torso while your palms are open and facing forward (the palms are aligned with the chest, and the back of your hands with your back).

- Adjust your arms to a horizontal position to the ground and your hands to the proximal level of your heart.

- Continue with your slow but rhythmic breathing, as you slightly tilt your head back and stretch to open your chest.

- Close your eyes if you feel stable, or focus on an object or a point in the sky, as you actively visualize your heart slowly beating inside your chest cavity.

- Try to visualize your heart function with as much detail as possible, as it is slowly but strongly beating in your chest and conducting the blood to your entire body.

- Hold this position as you breathe deeply into your chest, and slowly count your breaths (one full inhalation and one full exhalation = one breath) down from 11 to zero, while keeping the vision of your heart in mind.
    - You may feel a little tingle at the tip of your fingers in the beginning, but try to hold the position and count down from 11 to zero.

- o Slowly open your eyes or STOP if you feel dizzy and are losing your balance.
- Then lower your arms, shake them, and relax for a few seconds.
- Start a new breathing cycle from "the modified tree pose" with your palms on your lower DT and the same visualization technique.

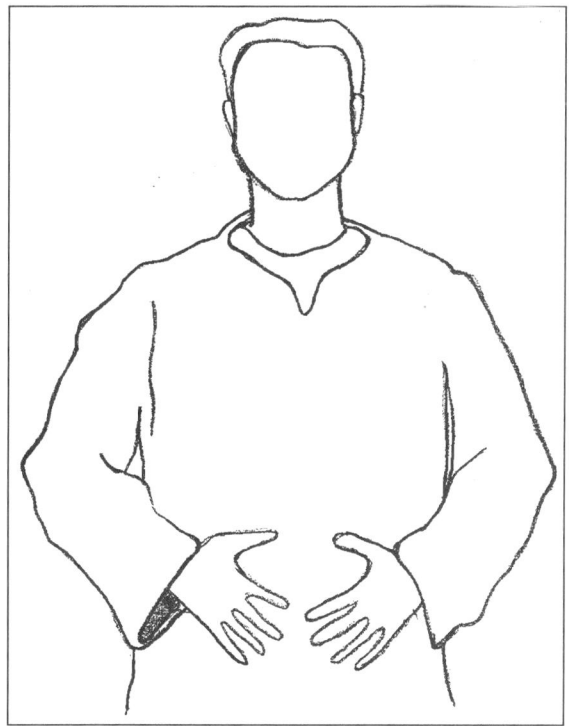

Modified Tree Pose (Heart Exercise)

- You should repeat this exercise 3 times, or until you feel calm and relaxed.
- **[EXIT PROCESS]**

   When you are finished with this exercise, slowly bring your attention back to the physical presence of your body. Feel refreshed and filled with vibrant healing energy which you have accessed from within your own body.

Remember that this is not only a physical exercise, but it's also an internal energetic exercise, so you don't need to breathe heavily or shake your hands too vigorously.

A major cause of panic attacks is the sense of losing control and not knowing what is taking place inside of our bodies. Many of my patients say things like, "I don't know what's happening to me when I am in a state of panic", or "I don't know why my body is doing what it does. My heart keeps racing faster and faster without any apparent cause, and it's hard to breathe", and "I feel out of control and disconnected from my body". Cases like these are prime examples of severe disconnection from the energetic body, the feeling of not knowing what is happening, and lack of control when they are in the panic state. The *Heart Exercise* will provide you with a direct connection to your middle DT and heart; as you repeat it on a regular basis, you will gain the ability to actually "control" and reduce your heart rate and blood pressure.

One analogy which I use to explain the mechanism of anxiety and a possible resulting panic attack to many of my patients is what I like to call the *Thermostat Analogy*.

The Thermostat Analogy

This analogy helps to explain the function of our sympathetic and parasympathetic nervous systems in relation to anxiety and panic attacks. Most people are familiar with a thermostat and know its function and general purpose. It regulates either air or water temperatures in a closed system (e.g., a house, or a specific room in that house). As you set the temperature in the room to 68 degrees Fahrenheit for the lowest and 76 degrees Fahrenheit for the highest, the thermostat's job is to kick in heat when the temperature reaches below 68, and pump in cold air when it reaches above 76. Its job is to "maintain" the temperature at a pre-programmed and comfortable range. This is called "*a negative feedback system.*" That means its function is to overcome the excess at either end in order to preserve balance. Now imagine a broken thermostat that produces heat when the temperature reaches 76, and pumps in cool air when it reaches 68. This is called "*a positive feedback loop*", which means that it works to exacerbate whatever situation is taking place rather than balancing it.

The "negative" and "positive" used in the thermostat analogy are purely engineering terminology. It has nothing to do with positive or negative energies discussed in this book. A negative feedback loop means a reaction which is the opposite of the current output, and a positive feedback loop means a reaction which is concurrent with the current output.

The basic mechanics of an anxiety attack are very similar to a broken thermostat. People may start to feel a little anxious because of any internal or external stimuli. These stimulating signals can be obvious to the person (like a motor vehicle accident, or winning the lottery), or can take place in the subconscious level (like a hidden childhood memory of abuse). Regardless of the cause, they start to produce the early signs of anxiety, like rapid heart rate (tachycardia), elevated blood pressure, sweaty palms, and shortness of breath. Under normal circumstances (a healthy individual), when their lives are not in danger and as they become more aware of their symptoms, their parasympathetic nervous system kicks in to calm them down and slows their heart rate and blood pressure (the negative feedback loop). However, in many anxiety cases, a positive feedback loop takes place, and the individual's body starts to produce more of the hormones and neurotransmitters which prepare them for *fight or flight* instead of calming and relaxing them.

This positive feedback loop will feed on itself and will continue to escalate and raise the "room temperature" (or the heart rate and blood pressure) to dangerous zones. The Heart Exercise will quickly activate our parasympathetic nervous system and start to reduce our heart rates and other vitals within seconds from the time we start doing it. Plus, the energy meridians of heart and pericardium, which are located on the anterior (inside) aspects of arms and upper chest areas, will be stimulated by doing the Heart Exercise. This exercise can also be helpful in cases of insomnia if it's done a few minutes before bedtime. Again, by doing these exercises on a regular basis, you can train your body to have better balance and react to any external or internal stimuli from a place of power.

Emotional Energy Transformation

LIVER *(Yin)*
GALLBLADDER *(Yang)*
EMOTIONAL CONNECTION *(Anger / emotional instability / Irritability)*

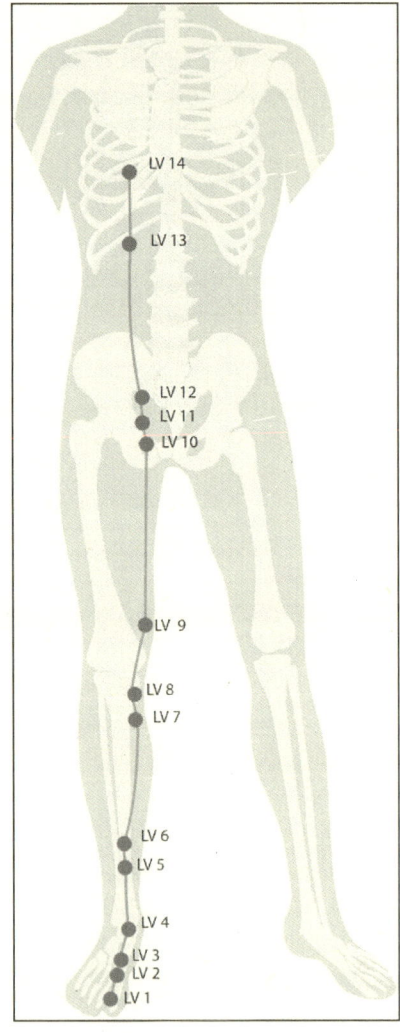

"Reprinted with Permission from - All-About-Acupuncture.com - All Rights Reserved."

Liver is a major organ in charge of emotional stability in Chinese Medicine. The main emotion related to the imbalance of this organ is anger. However, all other emotions related to aggressive behavior can also be linked to liver imbalance. Mood swings and roller-coaster movements of energy from calmness to an explosive state, and feeling emotionally unstable, are mostly related to this organ. It's also in charge of keeping what's referred to as "sinews" nourished and soft. Sinews can be translated to tendons and connective tissues. From that perspective, the liver plays a major role in relaxing the muscle and skeletal aspect of our bodies, as well as soothing the Yin element of the blood and calming the nerves. Thus, its imbalance will result in the opposite and can leave our bodies stiff and tight, and our minds uneasy. Cirrhosis of the liver is a common condition in people who abuse alcohol and drugs. It will cause internal dehydration by depleting the Yin element, and it also makes individuals more edgy and irritable.

The Liver Exercise is designed to soothe your liver and calm your mind. This exercise, and all others discussed in my book, will also help to promote healthy organ (in this case liver) functions, and help to prevent any negative diagnosis in the future. As I say to many of my patients, the "Best Medicine is Preventive Medicine!" You don't need to wait until you can actually notice these imbalances in order to do any of these exercises on a regular basis. Doing so will cause an ongoing internal healing response that will allow your body to react better to any possible distress.

The Liver Exercise

[Disclaimer]

As discussed in earlier chapters, you don't need to have any medical conditions to start using any of the exercises recommended in this book. You can practice them preventatively (in fact that's especially what I hope for), if you feel energetically more vulnerable, in relation to a specific organ or body part. For example, you can practice these exercises preventatively if you have a family history of any type of cancers related to the organ or body part, or if you partake in the type of lifestyle which might be putting that organ or body part at a greater risk.

Please consult with your treating practitioner if you are under care to treat any type of chronic conditions before you start any exercise regimen

Here is a list of *some* of the conditions corresponding to this exercise:

- Migraine headaches, dizziness, tinnitus (constant ringing in the ear).
- Anger management, temper tantrums, irritability, emotional roller coaster.
- Chronic alcohol use (two drinks or more, more than 3 times a week).

- **[Grounding Process]**
- *Find a quiet place and plant your feet firmly on the ground.*
- *Stand with your feet shoulder-width apart and your knees slightly bent.*
- *Relax your shoulders and neck, and rest your hands on your lower DT, and hold what's known as "the modified tree pose" (You can also do all of these exercises in a sitting position as well, as long as you are sitting on the edge of a firm chair with no armrests).*

- To start: breathe and raise your arms on either side of your torso, while your palms are facing toward the sky, as you inhale.

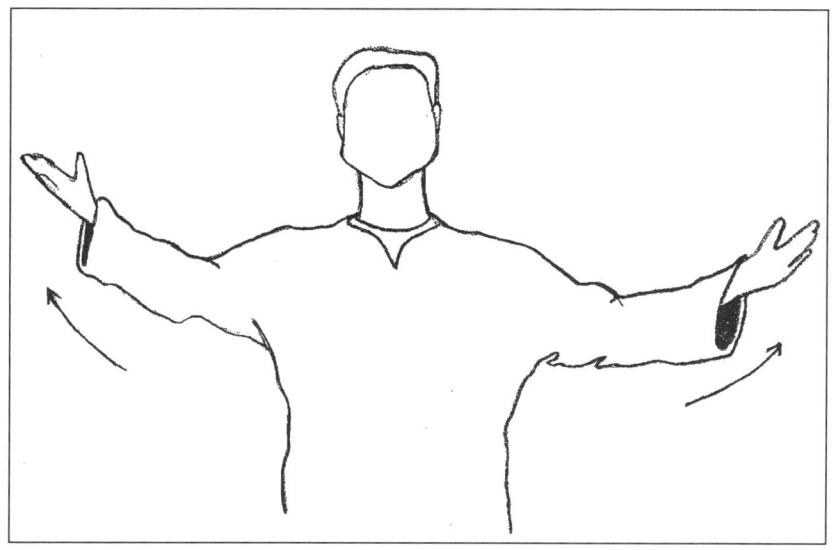

Raising arms (Liver Exercise)

- Raise your hands above your head to a comfortable height, as if you are holding a giant ball over your head.

- Then slowly bend your elbows; turn your palms toward your face as you slowly lower your arms in front of your face and torso.

Emotional Energy Transformation

Descending the arms I (Liver Exercise)

- Exhale to lower your hands while your palms are facing your body.
- Visualize that energy is descending down from your head, face, jaws, neck, and the rest of your upper body as you are lowering your hands.
    o I sometimes use a waterfall as a mental image when I visualize the energy rushing (pouring) down from my head to my lower DT.

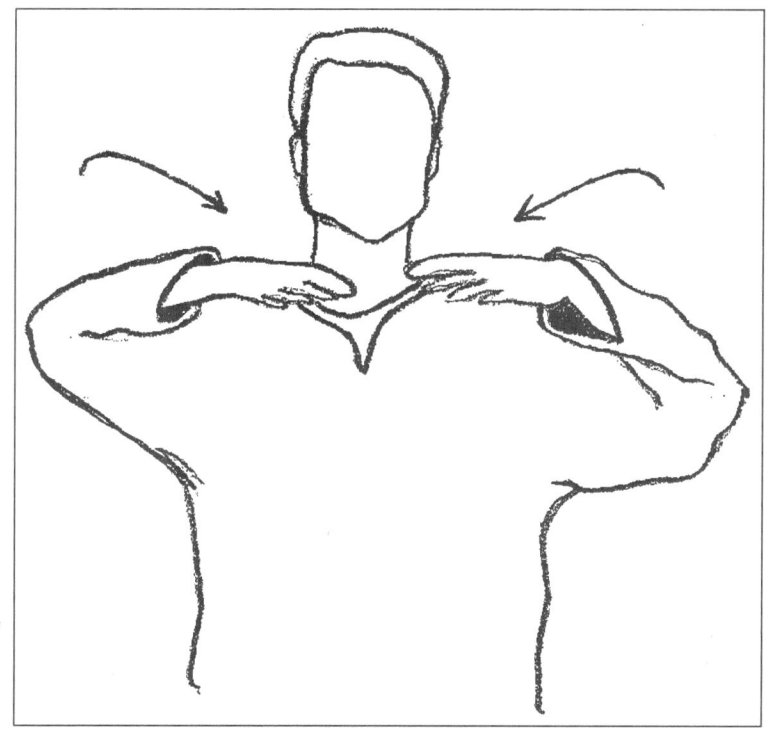

Descending the arms II (Liver Exercise)

- Hold your hands in front of your lower DT (don't rest them on your abdomen, just place them a few inches in front of your body) and hold this position for a few comfortable seconds (no more than 10). Breathe slowly, but deeply, while focusing on your lower DT.

Emotional Energy Transformation

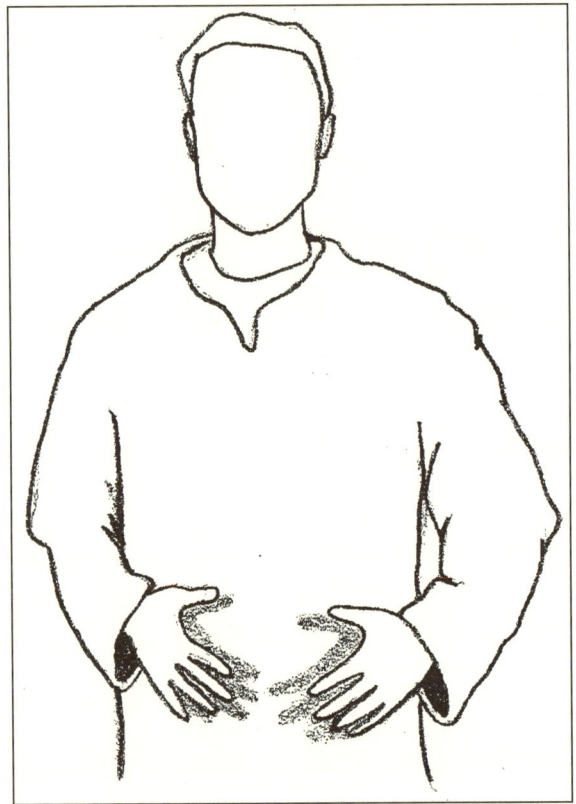

Lower DT Expansion (Liver Exercise)

- Then lower your hands slowly in front of your legs, with your fingers pointing toward the ground and palms facing your legs.
- Slowly reach to gently touch your index fingers to your big toes.
    - This is *not* an active stretching exercise; thus, you need to be very relaxed as you bend over to reach for your feet. Keep your knees bent and your body loose as you are focusing more on the progress of your movement (slow!) You can modify and go down only as low as is comfortable for you by simply visualizing a connection between your index fingers and your big toes. You can also do the same if you are at a seated position on a chair by just bending to your level of comfort.

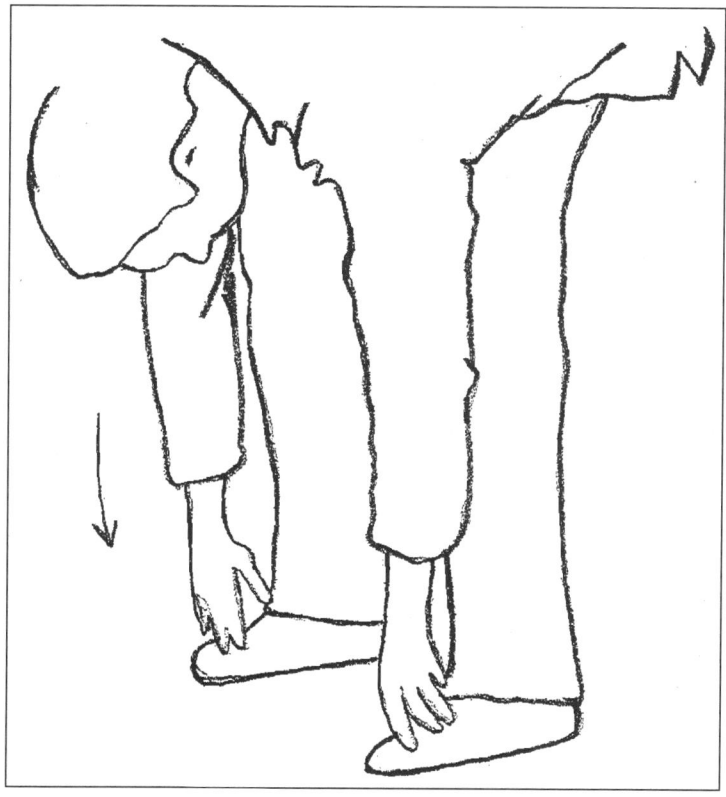

Touching the big toes (Liver Exercise)

- Slowly open your arms to either side of your body as you are raising your torso, and reach your arms back to above your head, as if you are holding a giant ball.
- Repeat this exercise 7 times. Breathe slowly to refresh your liver, soothe your blood, and calm your mind.
- **[EXIT PROCESS]**

  When you are finished with this exercise, slowly bring your attention back to the physical presence of your body. Feel refreshed and filled with vibrant healing energy which you have accessed from within your own body.

Emotional Energy Transformation

KIDNEY *(Yin)*
BLADDER *(Yang)*
EMOTIONAL CONNECTION *(Fear / timidity / sense of inferiority)*

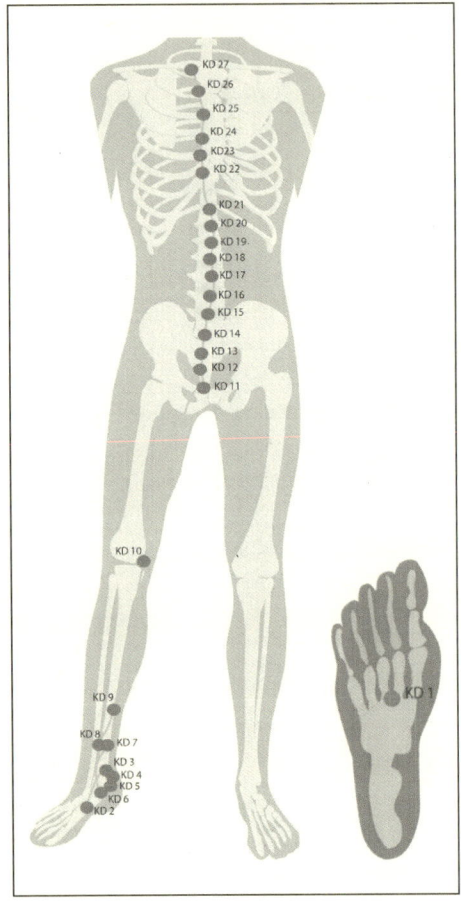

"Reprinted with Permission from - All-About-Acupuncture.com - All Rights Reserved."

According to both Western and Chinese medicine, kidneys are the main filters for all of our bodily fluids, which make them very important in regards to our daily functions. However, their role goes far beyond that in TCM, where they are also viewed as major organs for growth and development in the embryonic phase, and for aging in the adult life. For instance, early graying of the hair and hearing loss are conditions related to deficiency of kidney energy.

Kidneys are known to store a substance called Jing. This very important substance is the main source of genetic makeup in an individual. Kidneys are also viewed as very important organs when it comes to sexual health and function (especially in males). It is known that sexual promiscuity and overindulgence will deplete kidneys of their essence (the Jing substance) in both genders, and will cause early aging and chronic sickness. In Chinese medical text, this phenomenon however is mostly discussed when referring to multiple sexual partners and/or excessive masturbation. Kidneys are also known to be the gatekeeper of what's referred to as "male vital energy." A very famous acupuncture point, "Ming Man = the gate of vitality", is located roughly in between the right and the left kidney, and it is regularly used to treat male impotency due to kidney Qi deficiency.

The topic of kidney essence and depletion of its energy due to excessive sexual activity may raise many questions about sex and views of traditional Chinese medicine. However, that is truly a separate discussion and a book of its own. All I would like to focus on for our discussion here is that according to Chinese medicine, kidneys are closely related to human sexual function, and excess sexual activity will deplete them of their energy and essence (Jing). Now one might ask, "What is excess sexual activity?" The best short answer I can provide here is having too many sexual encounters without any close *energetic* connections to your partner will deplete one's Jing. The best Western interpretation of "a close energetic connection" would be a close *emotional* connection with your partner. Sleeping with multiple partners, and purely for the sake of having a physical experience (release), ends with the same result. Again, like everything else, this could also be relative to an individual, and their perception of an "energetic connection."

However, to put it in perspective, it is known within both the Eastern and Western medical communities that prostitutes (both male and female) tend to get many infections, which usually leads to major medical issues related to bladder, kidneys, rectum, colon, vagina, and other lower abdominal and pelvic organs. From the energetic point of view, this is mostly due to energy depletion and also what's referred to as "Murky Qi" in that part of their bodies.

Now, back to our main discussion on the kidneys. According to TCM, the energetic imbalance of the kidney organ is closely related to the emotion of fear and the sensation of shock from being frightened. The fear that is discussed here is not anxiety or worry; rather the primal and physical sensation of fear, when one is deeply frightened and shocked. Strong kidney energy (along with gallbladder energy) in an individual is also closely related to the sense of bravery displayed by that person.

This exercise helps when you are dealing with an emergency or a crisis situation. It will help you relax and calm down and make a decision which is not just a *knee jerk* reaction at the time of crisis. It also works well to build the kidney energy and creates a sense of vitality and promotes personal courage.

The Kidney Exercise

[Disclaimer]

As discussed in earlier chapters, you don't need to have any medical conditions to start using any of the exercises recommended in this book. You can practice them preventatively (in fact that's especially what I hope for), if you feel energetically more vulnerable, in relation to a specific organ or body part. For example, practice the exercise preventatively if you have a family history of any type of cancers related to the organ or body part, or if you partake in the type of lifestyle which might be putting that organ or body part at a greater risk.

Please consult with your treating practitioner if you are under care to treat any type of chronic conditions before you start any exercise regimen

Here is a list of *some* of the conditions corresponding to this exercise:

- When feeling physically frightened and shocked by an event or a memory.

- Stuttering, which was initiated by a fearful event.
- Bedwetting, excessive shyness, fear of heights.
- Kidney stones, impotence, UTIs, chronic (non-structural) lumbar pain.

- **[Grounding Process]**
- *Find a quiet place and plant your feet firmly on the ground.*
- *Stand with your feet shoulder width apart and your knees slightly bent.*
- *Relax your shoulders and neck, and rest your hands on your lower DT, and hold what's known as "the modified tree pose" (you can also do all of these exercises in a sitting position as well, as long as you are sitting on the edge of a firm chair with no armrests).*

- Start by visualizing your lower DT expanding slowly as you breathe.

Emotional Energy Transformation

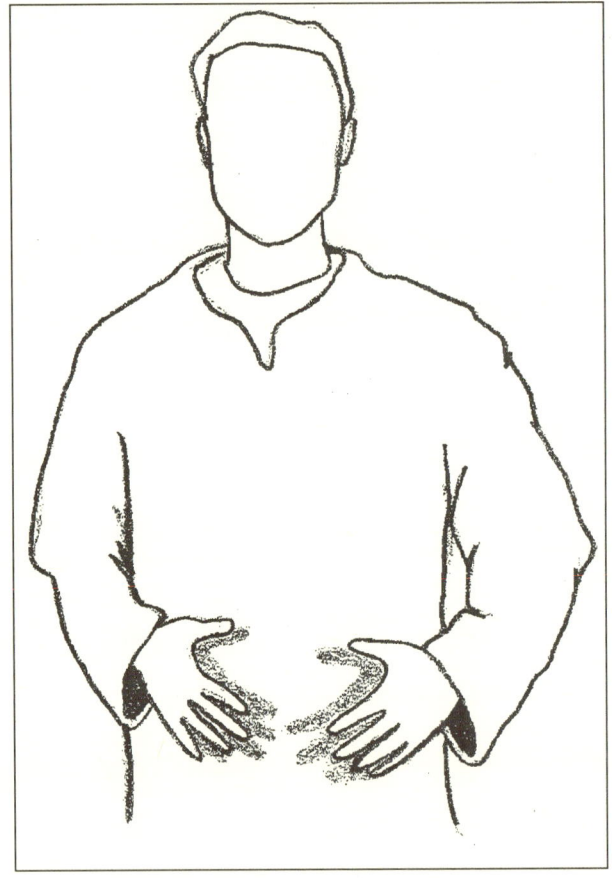

Lower DT Expansion (Kidney Exercise)

- Slowly move your hands away from your abdomen (about 3 to 4 inches) as if they are being pushed away by the expansion of the energy field of your lower DT.
- Visualize the energy field of your lower DT surrounding the entire lower abdominal area to envelope your kidneys.
- Slowly move your hands from the front of your abdomen to your lower back area, with your palms facing away from your back.

Moving hands from front to back (Kidney Exercise)

- Place your hands on your lower back with the backs of your hands touching and resting on your lower lumbar area. Relax your shoulders, elbows, and arms in this position.

Emotional Energy Transformation

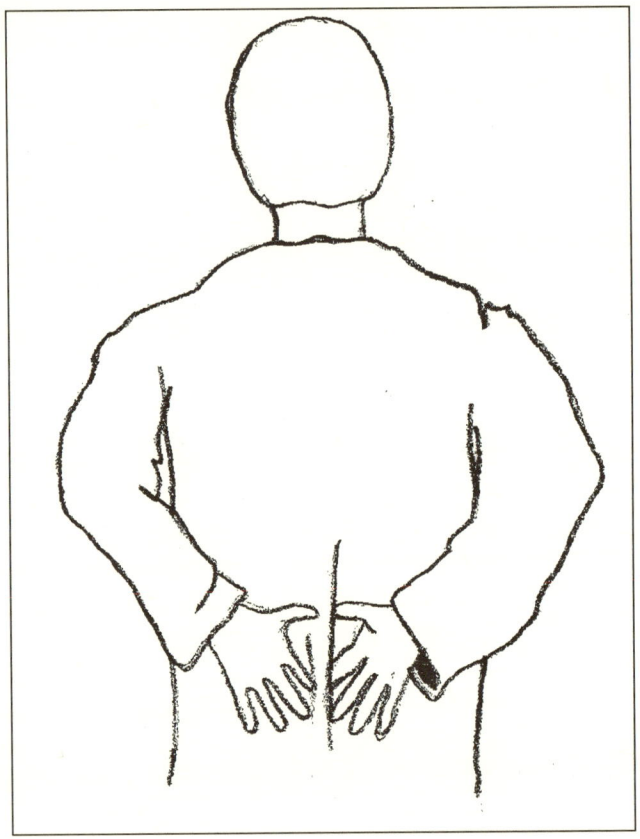

Resting hands on the lower back (Kidney Exercise)

- Hold this position as you expand your chest and breathe deeply.
- Visualize your breath traveling all the way down to your lower back and to your kidneys as you start to make soft fists and (gently) tap on your lower back with the backs of your hands (the dorsal area of your hands).
  - Keep in mind that this is *gentle* tapping, rather than vigorous pounding.

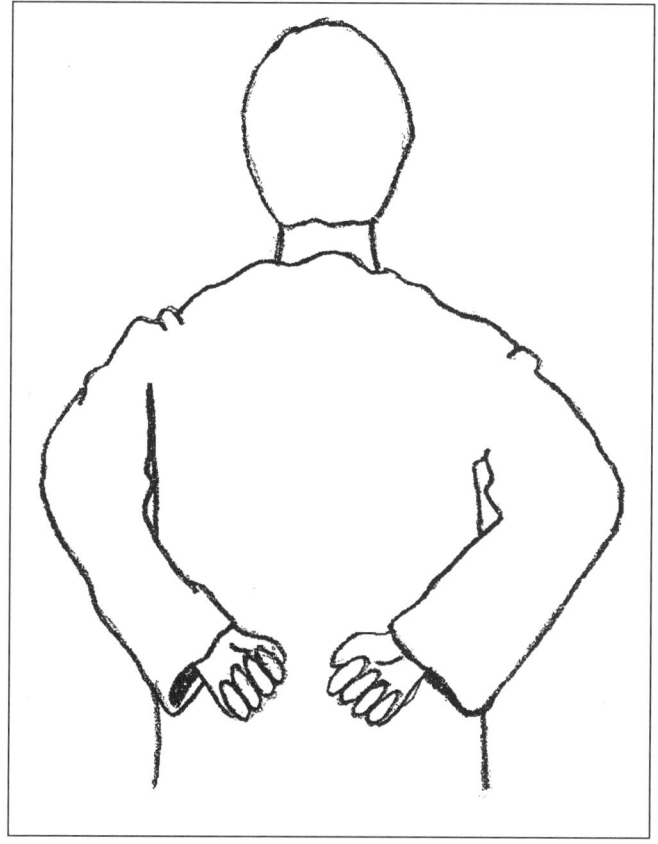

Tapping the lower back (Kidney Exercise)

- If you are truly and physically frightened, ground your feet firmly to root your body, while opening your chest bravely, and continue with the tapping.

- Hold this position for about 30 seconds, or count slowly up from 1 to 21, and then release your arms to rest on either side of your body.

- Shake your arms as you exhale aggressively (releasing big sighs of relief) a few times.

- **[EXIT PROCESS]**

Emotional Energy Transformation

When you are finished with this exercise, slowly bring your attention back to the physical presence of your body. Feel refreshed and filled with vibrant healing energy which you have accessed from within your own body.

If this is for maintenance, you just need to do the exercise once; if you are treating a KI related condition, or are in crisis and need to reduce the actual sensation of fear, do the exercise three times. This exercise will stimulate the kidneys and support the adrenal glands, which will provide you with a boost of positive energy. Like anxiety, fear is also directly connected to when a person senses a lack of control (feels powerless). This simple exercise will provide you with a combination of strength and centeredness when practiced on regular basis.

SPLEEN *(Yin)*
STOMACH *(Yang)*
EMOTIONAL CONNECTION *(Constant worrying and low grade anxiety/Sluggishness)*

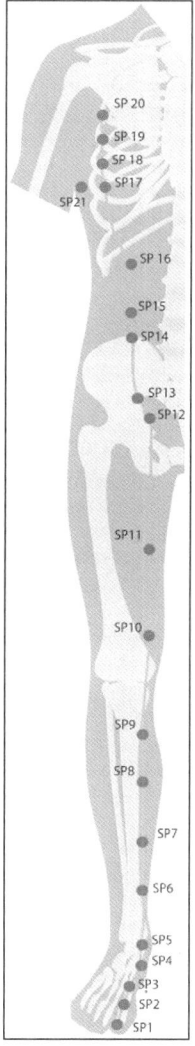

"Reprinted with Permission from - All-About-Acupuncture.com - All Rights Reserved."

Although the spleen doesn't have many known physiological functions associated with it in Western medicine, it is an important organ in Traditional Chinese Medicine. It has a distinct energetic role in regard to digestion and metabolism (transformation) of nutrients to energy. It also plays a major role in managing stress, and its imbalance causes what's referred to in Chinese texts as worry, or a low grade, ongoing anxiety disorder. Other references have been made about the emotional association between spleen and pensiveness, or sadness. However, from my research and the cases I have seen in my practice, constant worry and mild underlined anxiety are better descriptions. Imagine someone who is constantly worried about his or her siblings, parents, children, the economy, politics, the planet, etc. This person may not appear to be overly anxious, and many of his or her worries may seem to merit logical concerns. But it's the imbalance of constantly having something to worry about (being a worrier), which is mainly of concern here. This generally means that from the imbalance of spleen, we are more likely to produce and manifest these sensations of pensiveness and worry.

The opposite can also be true, not just for spleen, but also for all the other organs discussed earlier. Keep in mind that the emotional manifestations which were discussed in this book (e.g. anger = imbalanced liver), are manifested when there is an energetic imbalance of that organ. Thus, the opposite can also be true when the related organ is healthy and in perfect balance (e.g. peaceful = healthy liver). When the spleen is balanced and functioning properly, the individual feels calm and collected, instead of nervous and anxious.

The following exercise is designed to tonify the spleen and enhance its energetic function. That means we can expect to feel calm and worry-free after it's done. This exercise will also result in better transformation of our nutrients and help the spleen with producing plenty of energy. As discussed earlier, all of these exercises can be done preventatively. One should *not* wait for the imbalance to start working on the exercise. However, this exercise is specially recommended, for instance, when we feel overly tired and energetically drained, or when we are dealing with a constant, low grade anxiety and nervousness. This exercise allows you to collect your energy and center your mind.

The Spleen Exercise

[Disclaimer]

As discussed in earlier chapters, you don't need to have any medical conditions to start using any of the exercises recommended in this book. You can practice them preventatively (in fact that's especially what I hope for), if you feel energetically more vulnerable, in relation to a specific organ or body part. For example, practice this exercise if you have a family history of any type of cancers related to the organ or body part, or if you partake in the type of lifestyle which might be putting that organ or body part at a greater risk.

Please consult with your treating practitioner if you are under care to treat any type of chronic conditions before you start any exercise regimen

Here is a list of *some* of the conditions corresponding to this exercise:

- Digestive problems such as constipation, diarrhea, abdominal bloating and gas.
- Fatigue, diabetes, sugar imbalance, slow metabolism.
- Pensiveness, constant worrying.

- **[Grounding Process]**
- *Find a quiet place and plant your feet firmly on the ground.*
- *Stand with your feet shoulder-width apart and your knees slightly bent.*
- *Relax your shoulders and neck, and rest your hands on your lower DT, and hold what's known as "the modified tree pose." (You can also do all of these exercises in a sitting position as well, as long as you are sitting on the edge of a firm chair with no armrests.)*

Emotional Energy Transformation

- Start by visualizing your lower DT expanding slowly as you breathe.

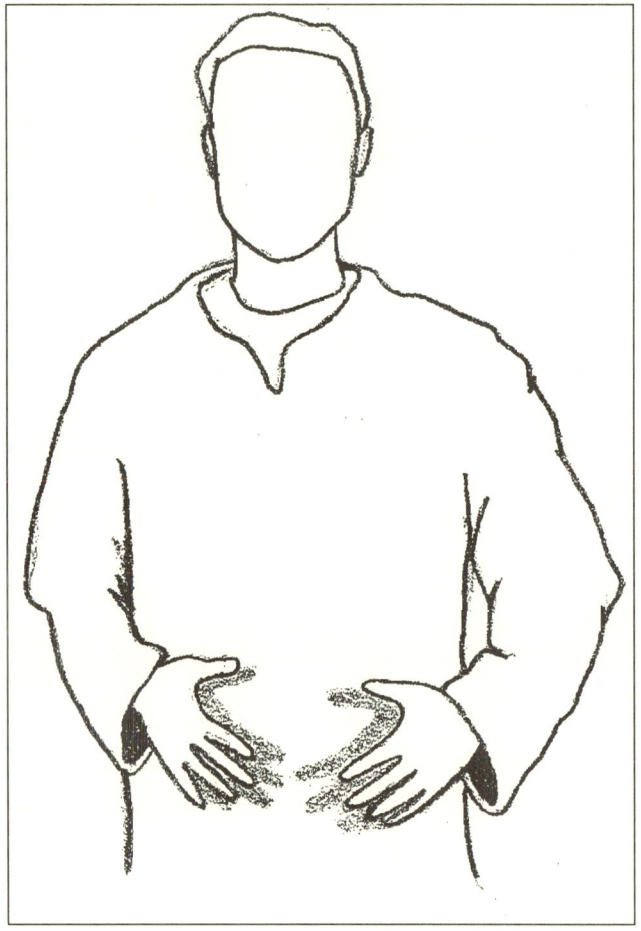

Lower DT Expansion (Spleen Exercise)

- Slowly move your hands away from your abdomen (about 3 to 4 inches) as if they are being pushed away by the expansion of the energy field of your lower DT.
- Slowly move your hands from the front of your abdomen to your lower back area, with your palms facing away from your back.

Moving hands from front to back (Spleen Exercise)

- Place your hands on your lower back with the backs of your hands touching and resting on your lower lumbar area. Relax your shoulders, elbows, and arms in this position.

Emotional Energy Transformation

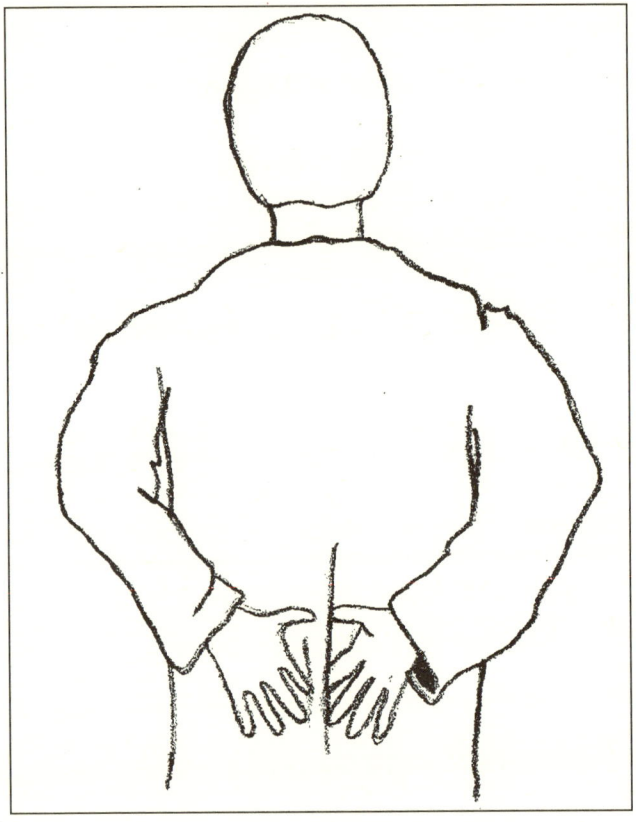

Resting hands on the lower back (Spleen Exercise)

- Start to make soft fists and (gently) tap on your lower back with the backs of your hands (the dorsal area of your hands).
    - Keep in mind that this is *gentle* tapping rather than vigorous pounding.

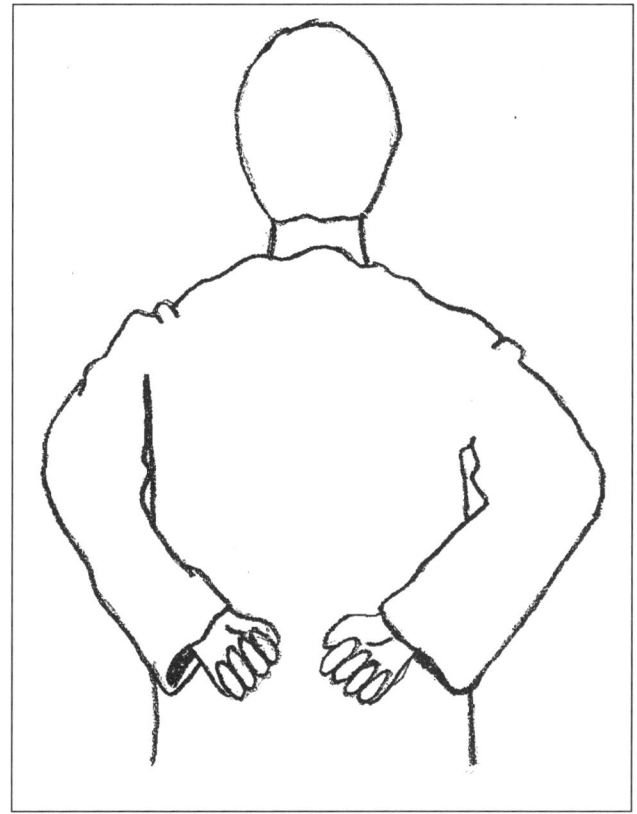

Tapping the lower back (Spleen Exercise)

- Now slowly move your hands to the front of your body while still gently tapping your fists to the sides of your torso.
  - Keep in mind that you can use any part of your hands, or fists, to tap on your torso. Just allow this to happen naturally, and don't *force* your body to do something that doesn't feel natural. Basically, use whatever part of your hands that feels natural and comfortable for your individual anatomy.

Emotional Energy Transformation

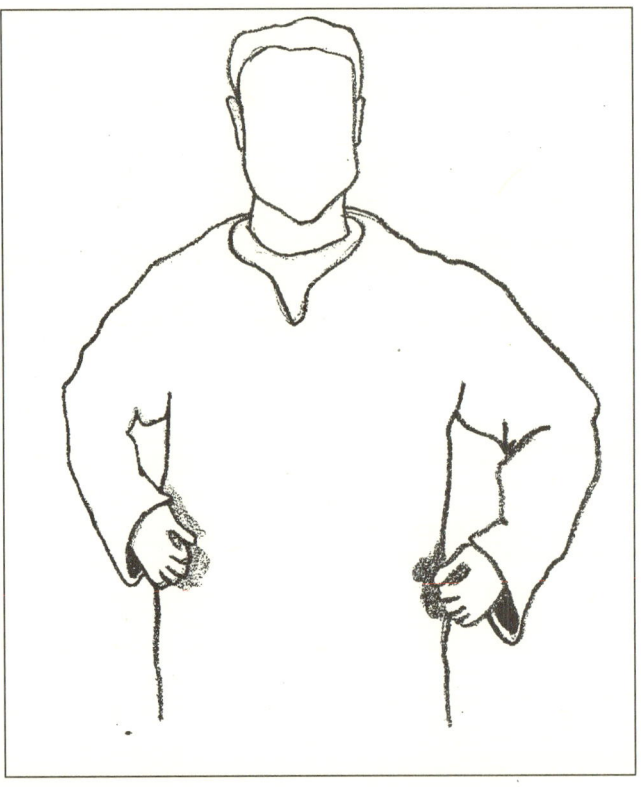

Moving hands from back to front (Spleen Exercise)

- Slowly move your hands forward as you continue with the tapping, until eventually you are tapping on your lower abdominal area.

- Now continue tapping as you slowly move your hands up and down on your abdominal area, but do *not* cross your diaphragm. This means do not move your hands above your abdominal cavity and onto your chest.

- Continue with this tapping process for about 30 seconds, or count slowly from 1 to 21, as you move your hands up and down on your abdominal area.

    o It's usually easier to create and follow a rhythm when tapping. It can be at any pace which is comfortable (natural) to you.

- Then, gradually reduce the speed of tapping and relax your arms on either side of your body while shaking them to relax.

- **[EXIT PROCESS]**

    When you are finished with this exercise, slowly bring your attention back to the physical presence of your body. Feel refreshed and filled with vibrant healing energy which you have accessed from within your own body.

Do this exercise once a day for maintenance, or repeat the process three times in a row if you are treating a related condition. This is an effective exercise if you are feeling tired (especially after eating lunch), and would like to stimulate your metabolism and energy transformation system.

Chapter Ten
Conclusion

There are other working models and different understandings of the human experience than the popular "Western" model. The Western analytical view of life has been discussed and researched, much more heavily in the last century, even by Eastern cultures. It does offer answers to many of our immediate questions. It has provided great advancements, especially in applied sciences and medicine, and has saved many lives in the past few decades. As I mentioned earlier, I didn't set out to criticize and undermine the Western thought process and Western medicine. I am actually a subscriber myself as a patient, and I advocate many aspects of Western medicine in my daily practice. I saw how Western and Eastern medicines can work side by side when I was working in Chinese hospitals. I am a firm believer in integrating Eastern and Western medicines to provide adequate tools and help every individual achieve their optimum health.

My intention in writing this book is to empower my readers by showing them their own untapped internal resources, and to introduce them to self-healing. I am opening the door to a new horizon and inviting you to experience new possibilities while providing you with a proactive approach to wellness. I am using what I have learned from years of research and practice to explain this new approach and to make it easy to be utilized. The simple exercises mentioned in this book will enable you to have access to a vast resource of internal tools, dating back long before our modern, Western *scientific* way of thinking.

The Western way of thinking is very effective for detecting and dissecting issues as problems that need to be solved. This approach is very effective when practicing triage in Emergency Medicine. For example, when a patient is dealing with a brain trauma caused by an accident, the practitioner needs to be able to quickly, accurately, and precisely detect and diagnose the problem to come up with a plan of action, since the patient may be hemorrhaging internally. However, when it comes to chronic and more debilitating conditions, the Western detective mind may not be the best course of action for treating many of those conditions in the long run.

A transparent example to demonstrate the deficiencies of the Western approach is the common treatment for an overactive stomach and/or an acidic upper GI with prescribing antacids. Strong antacids are prescribed prophylactically in most chronic cases without much consideration about their long-term adverse effects on the entire gastrointestinal system. I see many patients who end up with debilitating lower GI conditions like Irritable Bowel Syndrome (IBS) or Uncreative Colitis as the result of long-term upper GI acid suppression therapies.

Fortunately, more Western practitioners now have greater awareness about the long-term side effects of drugs they prescribe for their patients these days. More MDs would like to take the necessary time and talk to their patients about their lifestyle choices when prescribing medication to treat their conditions. However, due to the sheer volume of patients, pressure imposed by the insurance industry, and the pharmaceutical companies, many good doctors are cornered to practice fast, allopathic, and symptomatic medicine.

The general public and the patients are also responsible for making this trend of *symptomatic approached long-standing prescription* of medication more of a mainstream practice in the U.S. Patients are seldom educated properly; thus, they are not ready (and in most cases are not willing) to take control of their wellness and turn their lives around. Unfortunately, most people would prefer to maintain the status quo and rely solely on their doctors rather than taking the hard (but necessary) steps to turn their lives around. Intense pressure from the pharmaceutical industry has prompted many patients to think that "asking their doctors for medications" means being proactive regarding their healthcare.

To draw comparisons, the Eastern medicine approach when dealing with the same problem (upper GI acidity) is far more interested in its root cause than just treating the apparent symptoms. Examining the individual's life style, perhaps looking into less obvious and more subtle factors, can play a major role in the way an Eastern medical practitioner addresses the same problem.

The medical terminology used in Traditional Chinese Medicine involves multi-organs, and is based on a delicate internal balance between those organs. For example, heart fire may be causing stomach unrest, which was caused itself (the heart fire) by constrained liver Qi (energy) or a depleted kidney Yin element.

We rarely have "treatment protocols" in TCM, and we diagnose and treat every individual differently based on their constitution and their presented signs and symptoms. Two patients with very similar presentation of the same condition (peptic ulcer for example), will most likely be treated differently based on their individual imbalance which has caused the condition to manifest.

The Eastern understanding of life and wellness is based on observations of our surrounding nature, and it draws parallels between natural processes outside of the body and the functions inside. To the Eastern model, our body is a representation, a sample of the universe around us. The same order and energy which keeps the planets suspended at their precise locations, to cause or destroy life, also governs our bodies. The Eastern *holistic* philosophy believes that every event in the entire universe happens for a specific reason.

From that perspective, I believe that the outcome of every event which takes place in my life depends on my level of participation and intention behind my actions and reactions. Ultimately, the only aspect of my life that I have control over is the way I react to events that I am exposed to. That reaction will then set the course for any foreseeable outcome.

In relation to health and wellness, this simply means that if I am faced with any diagnoses, the choices I make in reaction to that news will set the course for a specific outcome. For example, if I find out today that I have high blood pressure (HTN), I can start taking medications and continue to live my life the same way, and face certain consequences, or I can choose to dramatically alter my lifestyle and *create* a different set of outcomes.

With the tools that I am teaching in this book, I am not only enabling you to add yet another method to the way you can address your health problems ***(Please consult with your treating practitioner if you are under care to treat any type of chronic conditions before you start with any exercise regimen.)*** I am also inviting you to take even one step farther, and become proactive when it comes to your health. Doing these exercises will empower you to be actively involved in matters related to your own wellness. You don't have to wait until you have an actual condition to do these exercises, remember: "Best Medicine is Preventive Medicine".

We are just beginning to understand some of the basics of this very complex system which we call *the human body* (I would actually much prefer to call it the "living experience".) To view and examine our existence from the *energetic* point of view, there are no differences between any of our organs, tissues, and other systems within the body. The same level (and quality) of consciousness which runs through our brain cells, is also present at the cells of our toes. There are no separations, just different manifestations of the same energy.

When it comes to our emotional health and balance, the Eastern philosophy is richer with stories and tales from the past. It's heavily infused with history, since the Eastern way of thinking believes in causology, and the real consequences of every choice we make in this life. Western culture promotes a greater involvement in the sensations which are felt at any given moment, and is seeking instant gratification based on what may be happening at that moment.

To illustrate this point better, let's take the emotion of *love* for a case example:

In the West, the emotional relationship that most young people associate with love usually reflects the way the object of love is making the lover feel in the short run. This type of relationship can be limiting and very conditional. It is more of a social/emotional contract, as in: I love you, if you love me back. And similar standards are used to masseur and evaluate the actual practice of loving between couples. The most intimate aspect of this type of a relationship is usually described with physical attractions (chemistry), and in sexual realms. Although these attributes are important, their contribution to the long-term health of a relationship is not paramount. They are the source of much fun at the beginning of a newly formed romance, but are usually unsustainable in the long run. This way of connecting to one another and using superficial measures to grade the intensity of your connection may be strong for a short while, but the intensity of this approach will almost always diminish as time passes on.

In the Eastern culture, love is mostly observed as an unconditional, deep, and an ever-present emotional bond. It is described (and sometimes desired) to be complex and multifaceted. Love's strengths and weaknesses are not measured by the level of sexual intimacy; its longevity is not based on the intensity of the physical connection between two individuals. Its strength is deeply connected with symbolic acts in relation to the devotion a lover expresses to display his/her act of loving.

In the very famous Persian love story, "Leili-o Majnoon" (Leili and Majnoon), written by Nezami Ganjavi (1141 to 1209) as a very long poem, Majnoon is deeply in love with Leili despite never having seen her close-up. He falls in love, and he remains in love with Leili for most of his life; he is dedicated to the *act* of *loving* and devotion he expresses to his lover without ever having a chance (or perhaps even dare to desire) of a physical encounter with her.

Western love builds a campfire under a teakettle, using a lot of dry and ready-to-burn wood; the water boils (and also evaporates) very quickly. It is a beautiful sight to see at the beginning, much hotter and more sensational, but very exhausting and often expensive to maintain. Its warmth varies and is fuelled mostly by the external factors and the behavior of the other party who is involved. Eastern esoteric love manages to slowly warm the water in the same teakettle through time, using the consistent warmth of only one small candle.

The point I intend to make in using the analogy of Western vs. Eastern love is to present two entirely different philosophies regarding one of our very complex emotions. Obviously, I am generalizing to demonstrate a point. I believe every individual relationship is different; I don't think that one size fits all, especially when it comes to love. The examples I mentioned are meant to demonstrate the two extremes in both situations. But sometimes, to form a more balanced view, we benefit greatly from "examining" both extremes.

Ideally, the approach to wellness which is provided in this book will empower you to become more proactive regarding your health and emotional balance. Like the teakettle analogy, I seek to provide you with a *consistent* source of ongoing balance rather than extremes highs and lows. The exercises offered in this book will enable you to approach your wellness and obtain greater emotional balance from yet another point of view.

There are different options to elevate your existence and to improve your experience than just taking medications. It may *sound* easier (and faster) in the short run to take the anti-anxiety or the anti-depressant drugs if you are nervous about your job or unhappy in your relationship. But all these emotional manifestations have underlying factors and are the indications of a deeper phenomenon taking place at the *energetic* level. We are usually conditioned and trained to block out that *inner signal* completely, and are promoted to live pretentious and *superficially* happy lives. But when you are unhappy, that usually means you need to reflect deeper and change your approach dramatically. Unfortunately in our society, it's widely viewed as less intrusive to fill out a prescription, or abuse drugs and alcohol, than to change jobs or to end an unhealthy relationship. The price we pay for all these prescribed or self-induced *suppression therapies* is the compromise of the precious and delicate physiological, emotional, and energetic balance within our bodies.

Through the self-empowerment exercises provided in this book, you can become *whole* with your deeper self and connected to your awesome *internal energy*. You will have crystal clarity with making hard choices when you are deeply in tune with your *inner voice*. You will begin to fully respect yourself and your experience on this planet, and will take your precious time much more *preciously*. The end result is the enhancement of the *human experience*.

Excerpts from Patient Conversations

Nick – 38 Y.O. male
Interviewed May 2008

Nick is a psychologist working in a rehab center as an addiction counselor. He came to me originally to seek help with anxiety and smoking cessation.

Siamak: Today is Saturday, May 3rd, and I am sitting here speaking with Nick. I just finished the guide to visualization: series one, and now I am going to ask him a few questions about his experience. So, first of all, this is the first time you have had this exercise in my office without having needles. Could you talk to me a little bit about that?

N: Actually, I got more out of it in a different way. I felt like I could concentrate more on the visualization.

S: When you were able to concentrate more on the visualization, do you feel that it changed your physiological experience of it as well?

N: I got more relaxed. And also this is how I have been, this is how I do it in my regular life.

S: I see

N: So, this is what I am used to doing

S: You find a quiet corner at home or at work?

N: Right.

S: Could you tell me a little bit about how you practice it at home or work?

N: I used to practice meditation in the morning for about five minutes and also did it for fifteen minutes before I went to sleep. I found that these exercises are easier than regular meditation, and they also make me feel better, even after I am done. So I have been using them instead, since you introduced me to them, over the past few months.

S: Ok, so you had your own routine for mediation; you were using a mantra of some sort?

N: Right

S: And with this exercise you have modified your meditation?

N: Right, right

S: And you feel like it has increased its effectiveness?

N: I feel calmer, and I feel like… I just feel like I am doing more.

S: What other benefits you have received by practicing these visualization exercises?

N: I am in the program of recovery from Alcoholism, and prayer and meditation are two very important parts of that. So I used to begin with prayer and then I ended with meditation. I have been more focused on these breathing exercises now, and the prayer begins to get me more connected with a "God center" as appose to a "self-centered" space.

S: I see. Since you mentioned this, do you mind if I ask you some more specific questions in regards to this exercise and possible connections with obsessive compulsive behavior?

N: Sure

S: Another way that I use these exercises is for some of my patients who come to me for anxiety disorder or treatment of addiction. These are individuals who may be emotionally unstable and get anxious and can't control their feelings, or patients who might be acting compulsively about a substance or a habit. I try to encourage them to use these exercises in those moments of anxiety or temptation, rather than being so scattered and taken by the moment. Have you been able to relate to them from this perspective at all?

N: Well, I do. Because I originally came to you for smoking, and although I still smoke, I am smoking about 75% less than when I first meet you. So, you know, I haven't quit entirely but I think it is helping.

S: You're able to control your impulses better, is that a fair statement?

N: Well, I feel like maybe the fact that I am more relaxed, that I am less stressed out, especially at work, you know. All I know is since I started the exercises and the acupuncture I am smoking much less and am feeling much better. You know 4 or 5 cigarettes a day opposed to 20 + a day, which is a big difference for me.

S: Yeah, that it is a huge difference. Any other impacts that these exercises have had on your life so far?

N: Well, I am a drug and alcohol counselor, and I have had a couple of clients who have asked me what are some ways to relax; I actually have gone through them with them in my office, and they have reported to me that it has helped them. So professionally it has, you know, it's something more that I can do with them. Other than that, it is kind of like I said, it has impacted my life because I used to feel that the meditation part of my practice was kind of boring, and now I feel like it's not.

S: More interactive?

N: Yeah, it's more active, and I also think that it is the discipline of maintaining visualization, I think it's stimulating. I feel like I am using my mind in a different way and feel more connected to my body. It's kind of a workout for your mind, but I am also getting relaxed and feeling connected with my body, it is hard to explain…

S: I understand what you are saying. Can I ask you a question about your connection with God or religion? Do you think in any way that connection, your personal connection with God and religion, is overlapping with these exercises?

N: Well, I'm not really part of any religion...I have a higher power which I have, over nine year of being clean and sober, developed for myself. I don't feel like the exercise has changed that. You know, since I am not part of a strict religion, I feel like it can fit within that very comfortably.

S: I understand.

N: I feel like meditation is to actually listening to what God says. And that can manifest in inspiration, it can manifest in sudden realizations, it can manifest in changing the way that you see an individual, or an action that you have done recently; I feel like any tool that I can use to get to that place benefits my spiritual life, and I am not really bound by any rigidity in that department. I feel like if this can make me calmer and healthier, then I feel like it is positive for my spiritual life.

S: I guess the reason I asked you is because some of my religious patients and I thought of this exercise, and I didn't know your religious background, and I didn't know that you don't belong to a church (I assumed that you did).

N: Right

S: But that may make your experience a little more unique. However, the reason that I ask you is because they refer to this Dan Tian as God or as Portion from God, or a reflection of God; they used their religious metaphors. I was curious about you and whether you had that type of connection or not with it. How or as what do you see it?

N: Well, I actually, when I have done the meditation I have actually felt that the energy might be something that God gave me. But, I don't see the connection so much. I feel more like it is a life force inside myself, as opposed to, um... an external sort of connection

S: I understand.

N: With God, I feel more like it is sort of a manifestation of my life in a concentrated way, um...

S: It is more a piece of you than something outside

N: Ah, a piece of me that is connected more to the universe in terms of like, a life force.

S: I understand

N: But in terms of my notion of God... my notion of God is too big to be a circle within myself that is glowing. I mean it's just not, and I don't have a conception of that, so...

S: Great, I think that you answered my question, which was basically whether you perceived it as a manifestation of your energy, whatever that is, or of it is something external outside of you... Well, thank you for answering my questions.

N: You are very welcome.

(END)

Elizabeth – 31 Y.O female Interviewed April 2008

Elizabeth is a college instructor and a patient who has come to me for a variety of conditions over the past several years, and I have used guided visualization and Qi Gong to help her. Recently, she had some specific issues around infertility which were helped with our sessions.

S: Elizabeth, can you please tell me a little bit about your experience while doing the breathing and visualization exercises?

E: It is very relaxing. I was more focused and able to concentrate better.

S: Are you able to easily follow my instructions?

E: Yes. I mean occasionally, you know, the internal dialogue does sort of click on, and it feels like I am mentally drifting. But, generally speaking, it wasn't that hard.

S: When you are mentally drifting, is it more like day dreaming, or more that you would be thinking about your day, or what you have to do? Please tell me a little more about that.

E: Really random, just kind of out-there thoughts or mental pictures. No, I wasn't really thinking about my to-do list.

S: Is it fair to say that you can physically and mentally relax within a minute or two after you start the exercise?

E: Yes.

S: As you are going over these breathing and visualization exercises, are you able to visualize your lower Dan Tian and your other energy centers? If so, can you please describe that for me a little?

E: Well, it is funny because sometimes I see it with different colors. Today I was really trying to focus on white and pure light. Sometimes when I think of the Sun, I think of it as a little more yellow, so the color can change slightly from time to time.

S: What other colors do you usually visualize the energy sphere in your lower abdominal area as?

E: I sometimes see it as a really pale blue; you know, like mostly white with a drop of blue. But, you know, we've talked, you and I have worked together in the past with other colors like green for rejuvenation and growth, so I've done green, too. And even sometimes when I listen to your voice saying that it's the size of an orange, I see a little splash of orange light.

S: That is a good point, because when I usually refer to the color of the sun I am referring to when you look at the sun directly, and from the earth you see a very bright sphere of light. Are you able to visualize your breathe travelling in your body?

E: Yeah, I think for me the hardest part is when I try to visualize my breath like a wave of energy. I can think of a fog, or a mist or something; I think of it without direction. So it was good when you gave me your directions and reminded me to think of it as sort of a powerful steam, like as if it is coming out of a boiling tea kettle. That image to me can be very powerful and forceful.

S: This is interesting because another patient of mine made a similar observation. She said that when she thinks of it as a steam, she is always visualizing this diffusing steam that can travel and expand in every direction. When you are visualizing your breath, are you able to visualize every single breath individually, or is it just one breath that you are following in your mind's eye?

E: Mostly every breath.

S: Okay, so you are able to visualize these waves that are coming one by one. Can you also visualize them going into different parts of your body, like your head for example?

E: That's somewhat challenging for me. I can usually see it traveling to my head. I can also visualize circling in my head, but I have a hard time visualizing all the thoughts leaving my head. I think, "What might happen? Could I speak? Do they come back?". So that's probably the hardest part for me, letting that go.

S: I see, so you may have had a little worry about letting go of your thoughts because you thought they might disappear and never come back again?

E: Yes.

S: Has it been easy doing these exercises on your own? And on what occasions? Or when do you feel like you need to do them?

E: I think when I need to relax and calm my mind, or of I am arguing or in the heat of the moment. In those occasions it is really good to just start breathing. You know, everyone says that you need to take deep breaths, but really just taking a deep breath doesn't do as much as these exercises. When I concentrate on getting connected to my own energy, and visualize my Dan Tian and breath as a wave of energy, I immediately feel more centered. It brings my focus inwards and helps me feel grounded. And sometimes I just remove myself from an intense situation by doing these Dan Tian breathing exercises without physically leaving the stressful environment.

S: Okay, good. Yeah, the heat of the moment is actually important. And one of the reasons that I want to teach this to people is because it could become a good tool to calm them down, regardless of the situation; even if you were in the middle of an argument, you could even argue more calmly.

S: The other aspect of this concept of energy cultivation and transformation is the effect it has on our emotions. What emotions

Emotional Energy Transformation

do you feel the most? Do you have any intense emotions during these exercises?

E: Not really. I mean, mostly I am very calm. I don't know if that counts as an emotion?

S: Sure it does.

E: I guess I get calm, then.

S: In fact, there is a belief that all emotions come out of calmness. They just transform. So the natural state of being is to be calm and feel blessed, and then everything else will transform out of this neutral state.

(END)

DJ – 28 Y.O male
Interviewed on May 2008

DJ is a young man working in high tech. He came to me with complaints from anxiety, insomnia, and depression. We just finished doing the first Qi Gong exercise "getting connected" a few minutes earlier. This is part of the conversation I had with him right after.

Siamak: How did you feel during the exercise which we just did together? Can you please describe that to me?

DJ: I guess it's hard because we went through progressive stages today. It's always easier for me to find my Dan Tian when you give me directions. I remember I had problems locating it before when I tried on my own.

S: So, is it fair to say that you were less in touch with your inner energy? Is that what you are trying to say?

DJ: Yes. I guess I didn't even know where Dan Tian was. I was able to—just with your guidance—sort of go into a lower brain state, and much quicker than I would be just if you were to leave the room for 15 or 20 minutes. I have to say this: I have never felt like this before. Once you described its location, once you started to tell me to start to focus on that point I got, like…a tickle… some sort of sensation right at that spot.

S: I see.

DJ: And I have never felt that before from any of the treatments that we have had. In terms of focusing, that was way more effective. Picturing the wave going through it was centering as well. I was getting to the point where I was drifting out but was still here…

S: Can you try to describe that sensation to me a little more, please?

DJ: Yeah, it's almost like when an organ or body part falls asleep, sort of the initial numbness.

S: Feeling numb?

DJ: The numbness—It's kind of like that, but it was deep—it wasn't like a surface sensation.

S: Um hmm

DJ: It was deep inside, it was right at that point. I won't say it was pulsing, but it was… no, it was like it was expanding.

S: Your lower Dan Tian, you mean?

DJ: Yes. It wasn't super strong, but I could still feel it.

S: So, when we talked about connecting your mind with your Dan Tian by using your breath, that wave of energy, the idea behind it is to figuratively descend your energy from your head to your lower abdomen. Could you tell me if you felt that as a physical sensation? Sometimes patients tell me that they feel a cold rush from their heads to their abdomen; sometimes they tell me they feel heat. Sometimes nothing, but they still can feel their minds are empty. Did you feel any sensations in that area?

DJ: I wouldn't say so… but it might not help that I just got back from the gym, ha ha…I don't know--might that skew the results?

S: Technically speaking, you should be able to do this exercise at any given time. The ideal goal is for you to be able to do this in a matter of a second or two in the middle of an ongoing situation. You know what I mean?

DJ: Oh, yeah

S: So, ideally you should be able to connect your Dan Tian at any point in your life experience and be able to use it as a source of groundedness, calmness, and a source of energy as well.

DJ: Now that you mention it, actually, before coming here, I was supposed to meet my girlfriend tonight. I had like some second thoughts about it... and like now it's like I am more certain of my decision, if that makes any sense

S: A-ha

DJ: Maybe more emotional stability. Yes, if I was able to do that in a conversation it would be really be easy to mellow out. I would say it is probably one of the most influential changes, or realizations, or shifts in perspective, or whatever you want to call it, in my life. It has been extremely significant, because once I started to understand the concept, then I started to be more aware of my own energy; then I was able to start controlling it, or influence its action.

S: Um Hmm

DJ: I am more cautious in my social interactions with people. And I would, for example, talk with some people, and my toes would become cold, and I realize that in the types of things we are talking about there is an exchange of energy.

S: Ok, so in the past, in the recent past, you were taking anti-depressants and anti-anxiety medications. How is all that, in relation to this work? Do you feel you have a new tool now to treat your anxiety and depression, or is it not doing anything for it?

DJ: Yes, I would say it is a tool. It's not a tool that is always easily accessible maybe; sometimes I forget the power of it maybe, or I am afraid... I don't know what it is.

S: It's easy to do that

DJ: Yeah, In general my symptoms have been reduced by like, 70% or something. It has been a while, but I guess the other thing is the choices that I make...I guess I am more cautious about the type of people I hang around with...After a good Qi Gong meditation, I feel lighter, and I feel like there is a little bit more energy, not a lot of energy like I just had a Red Bull or something, but there is more energy ... I feel more connected with myself, like I can look inside, I guess.

S: Focus? How about that? I mean, especially in your line of work. Is it helping that, or is it not doing anything for focus?

DJ: I would say it's helping, but that's also hard to say because now I have a bunch of people coming by my cubical and talking, and they are interrupting me. But now that I think about it, I am able to go back to doing what I am doing.

SS: And you used to have ADHD, is that right? How is it? I forgot about it...

DJ: Better; I mean, I'd like to say I don't have it.

S: Yeah, that's how I feel... Even at the beginning when we met, I don't think you had a lot of issues with it. I mean, a lot of itcenterson compulsive decision making

DJ: I guess the other thing would be that I am more cautious, like I have said, less compulsive.

S: You are more grounded and in touch with yourself.

(END)

Brenda – 47 Y.O Female Interviewed March 2008

Brenda is a cancer patient – third stage Lymphoma/Leukemia— who has been receiving care over the past three years, using many of my exercises to cope with different cancer therapies and their side-effects. We just finished doing the first Qi Gong exercise "getting connected" a few minutes earlier. This is part of the conversation I had with her right after.

Siamak: Was it easy for you to find your Dan Tian?

Brenda: Yes.

S: So, when you find your Dan Tian, do you feel anything initially, as soon as you visualize it—that sphere in your lower abdomen? Do you already feel something there? Or are you just visualizing it there?

B: It kind of happens at the same time. As I breathe more, the visualization becomes stronger.

S: Do you feel any weight any sensations in that location. Warmth, cold, anything?

B: Warmth, maybe. Nothing uncomfortable. It just feels like a focused feeling.

S: Alright, and then when I talk about the wave of energy in your body "traveling", can you visualize that?

B: I do, but I've gone through different points. I visualize more of the elevator-cylinder that goes from my mouth down, and so I tend to breathe that way. I tend to see it more like a cylinder in that I take a breath, and that connects me down further and to a deeper breath. So that tends to be an image that has stuck with me rather than a wave. But when I'm breathing, it's more of an up and down thing. But when we go in to spread energy into my lymph system, I see that wave, and I see what you're talking about with steam. I guess my breath seems more linear in that sense, because that's what I'm referring to with my esophagus and everything.

S: You are referring to an exercise we did earlier in which I used the elevator shaft as the analogy for you to connect to your lower Dan Tian. But the whole point is that you are able to connect these two points/areas in your body. You and I worked together before, and I talked about energy coming out and going through your lymphatic system. And that's what you perceive more as a defused wave.

B: Yes, because it's not as linear. And my lymphatic is throughout my entire body.

S: If I understood you right, you feel like the wave will move in all directions. It spreads and expands in all directions. So it's easier for you to visualize energy moving from your head to you lower abdomen like a piston, or an elevator in a shaft, because then it's not diffused, it's not going everywhere. It's going from point A to point B. Is that fair to say?

B: Yes.

S: One of the reasons that I described the wave of energy as steam escaping a boiling pot is because that's the Chinese character definition for Qi, "the steam that is escaping a boiling pot". When you were going through exercise were you able to feel your internal conversations slowed down?

B: Yes.

S: Do you think it's because you were visualizing this energy collecting your thoughts, or because you think you were concentrating more on your own body?

B: More concentrating on and connecting with my body. It's an internal focus, and that's what I'm trying to do, to calm my mind down in a meditative process. It's like a mantra, or anything else you do in mediation. When you're focusing on the breathing, it's intentional to get to yourself. So I am intentionally trying to calm my thoughts, by the breathing, by focusing on my breathing.

S: And how much do my instruction and voice play a role in this exercise? Do they make any difference?

B: Oh, it's a lot easier. Just like if you have your yoga instructor in front of you, it's a lot easier to do the moves the right way than it is to be on your floor by yourself in the morning. That would be what I'd compare it to.

S: When you try to do this at home, how long does it take you about to go through the whole exercise? Five minutes, ten minutes, twenty minutes? On average.

B: I am horrible with meditation, so when I try, it's probably about ten minutes, maybe 15. That is the best I really do.

S: We have been using this exercise while you were going through your cancer treatments; can you tell me a little bit about that experience, or more specific ways that this exercise became helpful for you?

B: There are times during treatments where you have to just sit in one space and let someone else do whatever they're going to do. Infusions, CT scans, MRIs—and so I have to relax, because I don't sit still well. That's when I use it. Also, a lot of my treatment has caused interruptions in my sleep pattern, so to get myself calmed down so I can sleep (or when I am awake and know that I am not going to sleep because I'm on drugs that are going to keep me awake), it's helpful to know that I can do some mediation so I can give my body rest because I am not going to be able to sleep a normal 6-8 hours. The other thing is that we have talked about the anxiety that is produced by having a negative medical diagnosis. So there are times when I have had, not anxiety attacks, but I can feel myself getting incredibly restless. So I can go in my office, turn off the lights, sit down, and do okay. I am going to do 10 minutes of getting myself contained and focused, and that helps. Anxiety, insomnia, and just being able to sit still and not look when they're pulling blood, or putting in transfusions, or adding chemicals or saline; you just have to sit still. And so those are times when I use these techniques to help me out.

S: These exercises that we have done together over the past 18 months or so, do you feel as if they have helped you change your general perception about cancer and life?

B: It has added to my tool kit the knowledge of how to deal with this diagnosis and its treatment. So, I don't know if I could say that it would be different if I'd never had the acupuncture, and the breathing, and the time with you and your friendship, and all the things we've had. I don't really have anything to compare it to, so I don't know how it would be different. I know that all the information has given me tools that I've used.

S: So you think it was helpful?

B: Definitely helpful and a good tool. Definitely something I would recommend to people, especially when you have a big change that you're feeling is physically hard to deal with. It's good to empower yourself so that you can change. With Western medicine, you just sit there and let someone else do something to you. It's good for my personality and my needs to have a level of control, of impact. You have a proactive stance that you're taking with breathing and visualizing, and it helps with accepting the situation as well.

S: A part of cancer diagnoses is a disconnection that patients sometimes feel with their bodies. Many people often get angry with their bodies when they have chronic or terminal diagnoses. They feel like their body is not cooperating with them. And they feel more and more apart from their bodies, rather than being close to their body or connected with it.

B: I think that's probably a cultural thing. I have done yoga and meditation over the past 30 years, and I've had a lot of body issues around weight and trying to accept how I am and what my body does. And so I am probably a little unique in that I have been more open to Eastern spiritual mediation and yoga. I don't know if I ever felt angry at my body for letting me down. You know, it's just, it felt unfair, but part of it is, "Well, maybe I'm better equipped to handle this than someone else". It wasn't like why me, it was like why *not* me. You know, 1 in 3 people are going to have this, so I guess I'm better equipped to handle this than so-and-so. Or maybe I have better resources.

S: That's probably the case. A big part of this exercise is to provide a tool to be able to feel your body and connect with it better, on a different level that you have not done before. Usually in Western culture, the closest way people relate and connect is by looking at themselves in the mirror. This is an exercise for people to really get connected to their bodies on an energetic level. Do you think it has helped you to achieve that?

B: Yes.

S: Would you like to add anything?

B: I think the thing that helps me the most is the idea of empowering and the issue of anxiety, and I think those are tied together. We isolate ourselves because we have anxiety, and we don't want to share that with people or take responsibility for things. But if you do, and you have these kinds of tools, I think it makes it a lot easier to cope and balance everyday life. So that's when I feel these exercises are great tools and coping mechanisms.

(END)